STEPHEN BIESTY'S
INCREDIBLE
BODY
CROSS-SECTIONS

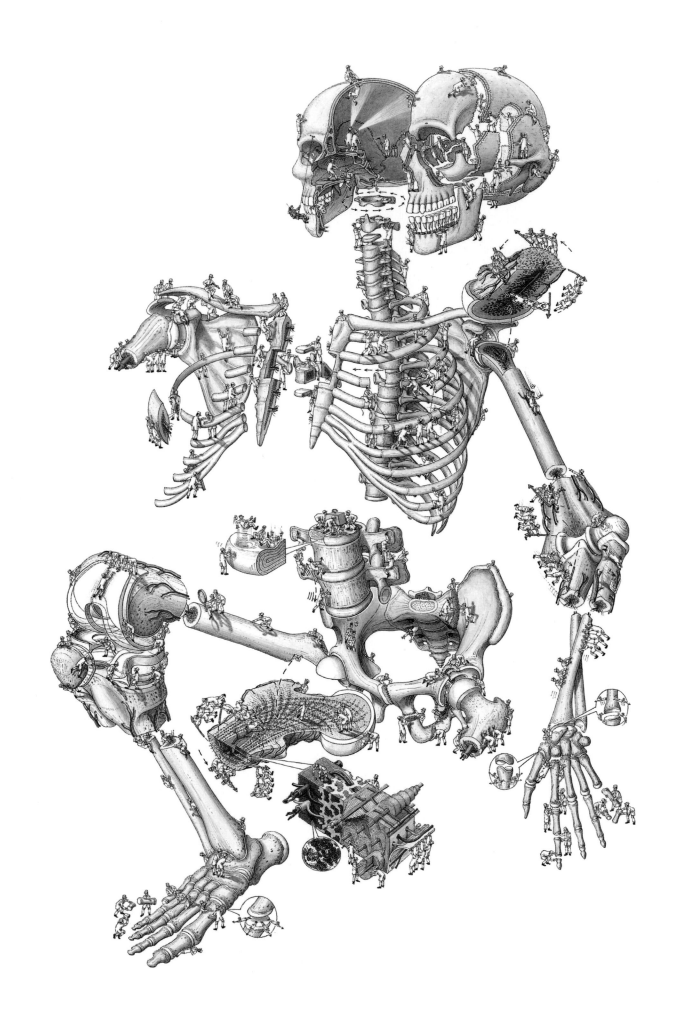

STEPHEN BIESTY'S
INCREDIBLE
BODY
CROSS-SECTIONS

ILLUSTRATED BY
STEPHEN BIESTY

WRITTEN BY
RICHARD PLATT

DK

FIRST EDITION
Project Editors Mary Atkinson, Francesca Baines
Senior Art Editors Peter Radcliffe, Dorian Spencer Davies
Senior Editor Scarlett O'Hara
Senior Managing Editor Linda Martin
Medical Consultant Gabrielle Murphy
DTP Designer Almudena Díaz
Production Lisa Moss

REVISED EDITION
Senior Editors Ann Baggaley, Rupa Rao **Senior Art Editor** Rachael Grady
Managing Editors Francesca Baines, Kingshuk Ghoshal
Managing Art Editors Philip Letsu, Govind Mittal
US Editor Megan Douglass **US Executive Editor** Lori Cates Hand
Senior DTP Designer Sachin Singh
DTP Designers Pawan Kumar, Dheeraj Singh, Bimlesh Tiwary
Pre-Production Manager Balwant Singh
Production Manager Pankaj Sharma
Production Editor Jacqueline Street
Senior Production Controller Jude Crozier
Jacket Designer Akiko Kato
Jacket Design Development Manager Sophia MTT
Publisher Andrew Macintyre **Associate Publishing Director** Liz Wheeler
Art Director Karen Self **Publishing Director** Jonathan Metcalf

This American Edition, 2020
First American Edition, 1998
Published in the United States by DK Publishing
1450 Broadway, Suite 801, New York, NY 10018

Illustrations copyright © 1998, 2017, 2020 Stephen Biesty
Text copyright © 1998, 2017, 2020 Richard Platt
Compilation copyright © 1998, 2017, 2020 Dorling Kindersley Limited
DK, a Division of Penguin Random House LLC
20 21 22 23 24 10 9 8 7 6 5 4 3 2 1
001-316000-Aug/2020

A catalog record for this book is available from the Library of Congress.
ISBN 978-1-4654-9145-9

DK books are available at special discounts when purchased in bulk
for sales promotions, premiums, fund-raising, or educational use.
For details, contact: DK Publishing Special Markets,
1450 Broadway, Suite 801, New York, NY 10018
SpecialSales@dk.com

Printed and bound in China

For the curious

www.dk.com

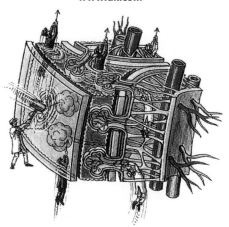

CONTENTS

A JOURNEY OF DISCOVERY
6

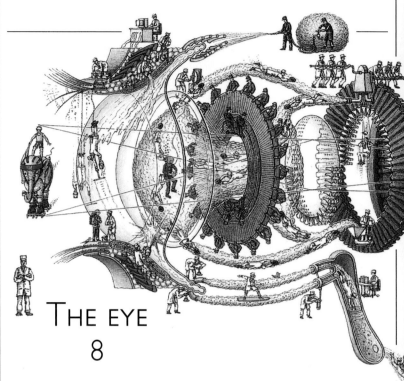

THE EYE
8

THE EAR
10

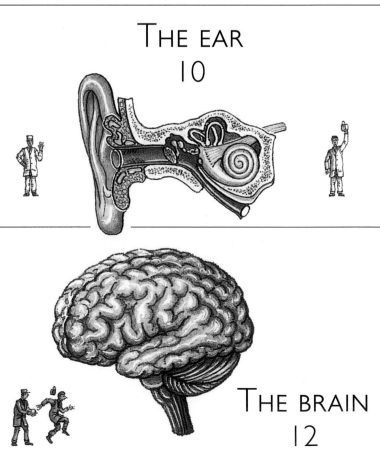

THE BRAIN
12

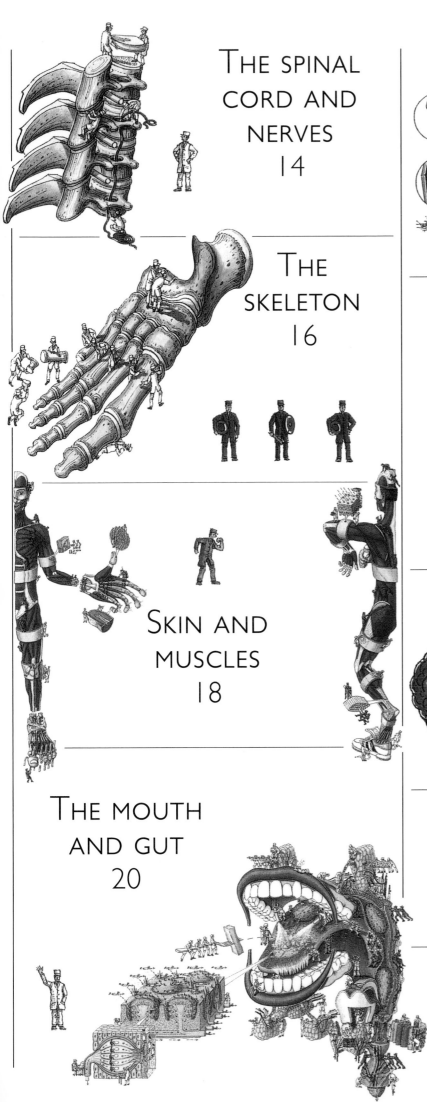
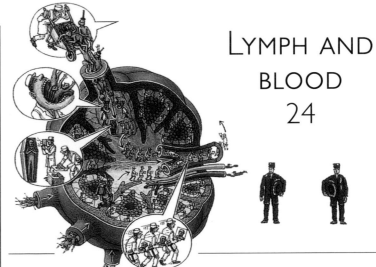
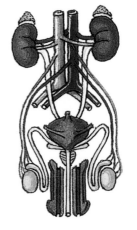

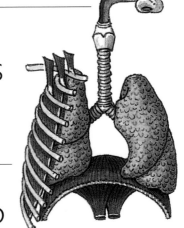

A journey of discovery

"EXTRAORDINARY EXPLORATION SQUAD reporting for duty! Our mission: to explore and map every corner of an unknown territory—the human body. The chosen subject: Stephen Biesty; gender—male; profession—artist. We have trained for months for this unique expedition and are prepared for every obstacle—we will wriggle through the tiniest vein, or leap through a pore of his skin. We're equipped for almost any situation, with scuba equipment, mountaineering gear, and hurricane-proof jackets. Steve's body is always hot, so we won't need any thermal underwear. But we have two-way radios so that we can communicate with each other. Fast-flowing pipelines and high-speed nerve highways connect every limb and organ of Steve's body, so traveling around should be easy. We estimate that we'll complete our mission in roughly 24 pages."

The eyes

A miracle of miniaturization, Steve's eyes are more powerful than the most advanced movie camera. Six muscles turn each eye so that he can look in many directions. A bundle of nerve fibers carries signals from his eyes to his brain, where the impulses are interpreted as images (pp.8–9).

Skin and muscles

Steve's skin is his largest organ. It provides a physical barrier, prevents him from getting too hot or cold, and gives him a sense of touch. The "meat" on Steve's bones is muscle tissue. As well as allowing Steve to move parts of his body, muscles help keep his body warm (pp.18–19).

The lungs

When Steve breathes in, oxygenated air inflates his lungs. Blood circulating in the lungs exchanges waste gases for the oxygen. When he breathes out, Steve can use the exhaled air to talk or sing (pp.30–31).

The brain

Protected by a hollow ball of bone, Steve's brain is the control center of his body. The cerebrum, the largest part of the brain, enables Steve to think. It is divided into two halves called hemispheres. Different parts of the cerebral hemispheres, and other parts of the brain, interpret messages from his senses, control movement, and work automatically to keep his heart beating (pp.12–13).

The ears

Steve's ears allow him to enjoy loud rock music—or hear a pin drop. They also have another important function. Fluid flowing in curved, bony tubes deep inside the ear gives Steve a sense of balance, so that he can stand upright and walk without falling over (pp.10–11).

The spinal cord

Running straight down his back inside a flexible, bony tube (the vertebral column), Steve's spinal cord keeps his brain in touch with nerves throughout his body (pp.14–15).

The heart

Although no bigger than his fist, Steve's heart is a hard-working, powerful pump. It squeezes and relaxes constantly to circulate blood around his body (pp.28–29).

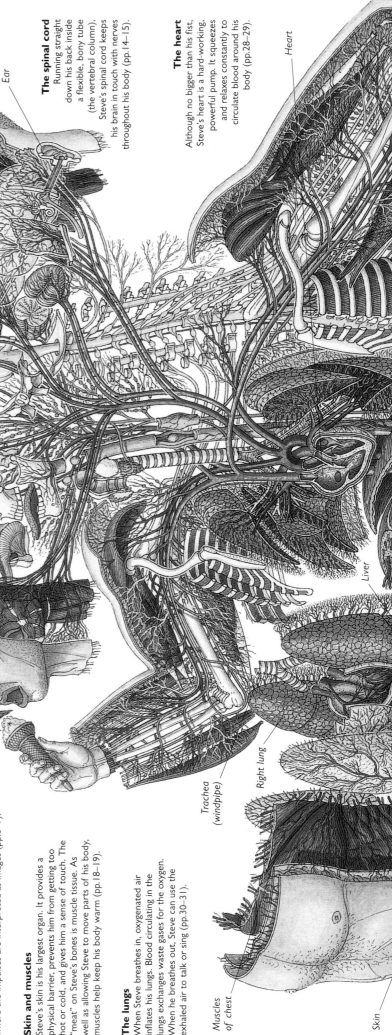

Organs of balance

Ear

Left cerebral hemisphere

Skull

Right cerebral hemisphere

Eye

Heart

Liver

Right lung

Trachea (windpipe)

Muscles of chest

Skin

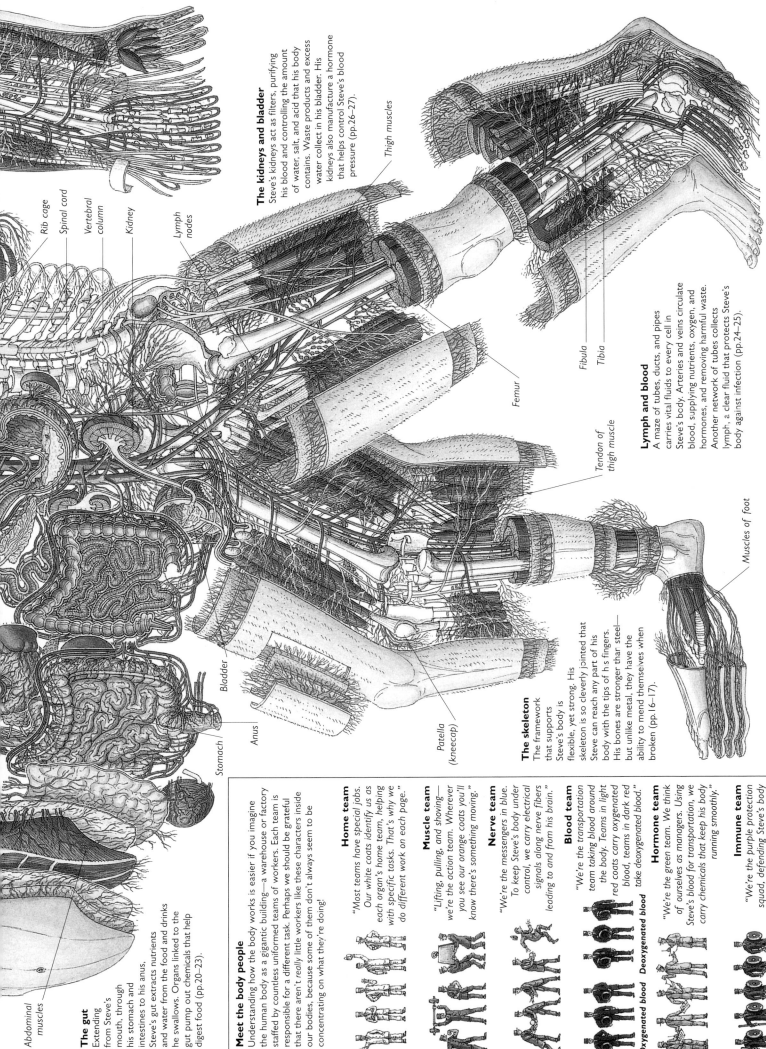

The kidneys and bladder
Steve's kidneys act as filters, purifying his blood and controlling the amount of water, salt, and acid that his body contains. Waste products and excess water collect in his bladder. His kidneys also manufacture a hormone that helps control Steve's blood pressure (pp.26–27).

Thigh muscles

Rib cage

Spinal cord

Vertebral column

Kidney

Lymph nodes

Femur

Fibula

Tibia

Tendon of thigh muscle

Lymph and blood
A maze of tubes, ducts, and pipes carries vital fluids to every cell in Steve's body. Arteries and veins circulate blood, supplying nutrients, oxygen, and hormones, and removing harmful waste. Another network of tubes collects lymph, a clear fluid that protects Steve's body against infection (pp.24–25).

Muscles of foot

Patella (kneecap)

The skeleton
The framework that supports Steve's body is flexible, yet strong. His skeleton is so cleverly jointed that Steve can reach any part of his body with the tips of his fingers. His bones are stronger than steel—but unlike metal, they have the ability to mend themselves when broken (pp.16–17).

Bladder

Anus

Stomach

Abdominal muscles

The gut
Extending from Steve's mouth, through his stomach and intestines to his anus, Steve's gut extracts nutrients and water from the food and drinks he swallows. Organs linked to the gut pump out chemicals that help digest food (pp.20–23).

Meet the body people
Understanding how the body works is easier if you imagine the human body as a gigantic building—a warehouse or factory staffed by countless uniformed teams of workers. Each team is responsible for a different task. Perhaps we should be grateful that there aren't really little workers like these characters inside our bodies, because some of them don't always seem to be concentrating on what they're doing!

Home team
"Most teams have special jobs. Our white coats identify us as each organ's home team, helping with specific tasks. That's why we do different work on each page."

Muscle team
"Lifting, pulling, and shoving—we're the action team. Wherever you see our orange coats you'll know there's something moving."

Nerve team
"We're the messengers in blue. To keep Steve's body under control, we carry electrical signals along nerve fibers leading to and from his brain."

Blood team
"We're the transportation team taking blood around the body. Teams in light red coats carry oxygenated blood, teams in dark red take deoxygenated blood."

Oxygenated blood   Deoxygenated blood

Hormone team
"We're the green team. We think of ourselves as managers. Using Steve's blood for transportation, we carry chemicals that keep his body running smoothly."

Immune team
"We're the purple protection squad, defending Steve's body against attack from bacteria and viruses that could make him ill."

The eye

STARTING OUR JOURNEY seemed easy: we planned to climb into Steve's mouth. But as we scaled his face, a hurricane-force wind plucked us into the air and sucked us up his nose. The sneeze that followed blasted us down a dark, narrow corridor, knocking us both unconscious. When we came around, we thought at first we were in a cinema. The domed ceiling and floor were vivid red. Behind us a giant lens projected a moving picture onto the wall, but the image was upside down! Then it dawned on us—we had reached an eye through Steve's tear duct. Struggling out the same way, we saw cleaners at work. As we watched them, one gave us a message. "Take this impulse up the optic nerve to Steve's brain," he said, "and watch out for those follicle mites. They can give you a nasty bite."

Egyptian eyewash
Ancient Egyptians used urine for eyewash. Other eye treatments included the droppings of flies, pelicans, lizards, or crocodiles.

"Wow! These fibers are so stretchy, you could make elastic bands from them!"

Eyelids
Eyelids protect the eyes and spread tears across them to wash them. Eyelashes keep sweat and dust out of Steve's eyes.

Water bed
Between the lens and the cornea is a clear liquid called aqueous fluid. It holds the lens in place and keeps the cornea in shape.

"Hey guys, let's do a squint!"

"We work in Steve's tear glands, making tears to clean and lubricate his eyes."

"Our pumping replaces all the aqueous fluid 16 times a day."

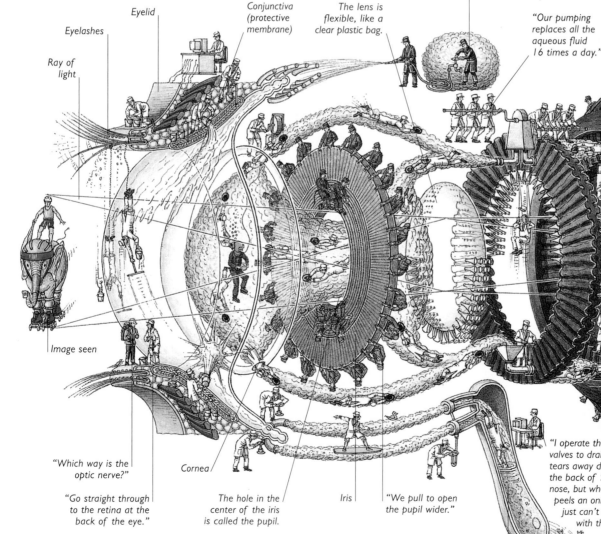

Conjunctiva (protective membrane)

The lens is flexible, like a clear plastic bag.

Eyelid

Eyelashes

Ray of light

Image seen

"Which way is the optic nerve?"

"Go straight through to the retina at the back of the eye."

Cornea

The hole in the center of the iris is called the pupil.

Iris

"We pull to open the pupil wider."

"I operate the valves to drain tears away down the back of Steve's nose, but when he peels an onion, I just can't cope with the flow."

Tear duct

"Waagh!"

1. Sharp pictures
Seeing starts at the cornea, a clear window at the front of Steve's eyes. Beams of light bend as they pass through the cornea and the fluid-filled chamber behind it. The bending focuses the light, gathering the rays so that they form a clear picture on the eye's inner surface.

2. Adjusting brightness
Next, the light passes through the hole in the center of the colored part of Steve's eye, a muscular ring called the iris. In bright light, the muscle tightens, narrowing the hole in the middle. This reduces the amount of light entering the eye, so Steve isn't dazzled.

3. Seeing far and near
Behind the iris, a lens helps Steve see far and near things equally clearly. To focus on close things, Steve tightens his eye muscles. This makes the lens bulge, bending light rays strongly. Light rays from distant objects need less bending. So Steve relaxes his eye muscles, allowing the rubbery fibers to stretch the lens into a flatter shape that bends light less.

Sight problems

Long-sighted people have eyeballs that are too short, and need glasses to see nearby objects. Short-sighted people have egg-shaped eyeballs and can't see distant objects without glasses. Steve doesn't need glasses, but a quarter of all children wear them, as do most grandparents.

Eagle eyes

Steve's eyes are sharp enough to pick out a golf ball at a distance of 1,500 yards (1.4 km), but he's not unusual. Most of us can see this well, though we may need glasses to make the most of our remarkable vision.

"This spongy layer of fat provides soft, protective padding for Steve's eyeball."

"This squishy jelly gives the eye its circular shape and holds the retina in place. Light passes straight through it."

Rod cells

One hundred and twenty million rod-shaped cells enable Steve to see shapes and movement. They work even in the dimmest starlight.

Cone cells

The six million cone-shaped cells work in bright light only. They detect colors and give Steve a clearer picture of objects he studies closely.

5. Seeing cells

Light falling on the retina activates special cells shaped like rods and cones. The cells send tiny impulses down nerve fibers linking the eye and brain. Steve's brain (pp.12–13) processes the nerve signals, turning them into a picture that Steve can understand.

Cone cell   Rod cell

Upside-down image on Steve's retina of the elephant that he is looking at

"There are three pairs of muscles for each of Steve's eyes. Between us we can rotate his eyeball, and roll it up and down, or from left to right."

Sclera (white of the eye)

Sclera (white of the eye)

"We swim along the arteries to keep them supplied with blood rich in oxygen and nutrients."

"We're the fastest-reacting muscles in Steve's body!"

"I'm off to Steve's brain!"

The optic nerve is made up of about a million nerve fibers, linking the eye to the brain and enabling Steve to see moving images instantaneously.

4. Projecting the picture

The inside of the eye works like a camera. The lens projects a sharp image onto the back surface of the eye. There, a layer of light-sensitive cells called the retina works like photographic film. The image on the retina is upside down, but Steve's brain (pp.12–13) will turn it the right way up.

The blind spot

Everyone's retina has a "blind spot" where there are no nerve cells for seeing. The blind spot is the point where nerve fibers from all over the retina gather together to form the optic nerve.

The ear

FEELING OUR WAY along a shiny bundle of nerve fibers, we squeezed through a small, circular hole where the fibers branched. Should we take the left or the right fork? We tossed a coin and chose the left. It led to a narrow tunnel, like the inside of a seashell. Baffled, we consulted our map. Only one part of Steve's body looked like this: the inner ear. The spiraling, liquid-filled tube changes sound waves into nerve impulses. The air-filled middle ear contains tiny bones that conduct sound. These delicate mechanisms are hidden away deep inside Steve's head. The crumpled flaps of cartilage on the sides of his head that we call ears do not do the hearing. They funnel sound down a short tube that leads to the middle ear.

Positive identification
Steve's outer ear is unique: nobody else's looks quite the same. Its shape began to form before Steve was born, but has not changed since his first birthday. In fact, forensic scientists have suggested using ear shape to identify criminals who wear masks that cover only the front of their heads.

"Hey! can you 'ear me? The pinna (outer ear) is shaped to collect and guide sound into Steve's external auditory canal."

"We're riding on the sound waves traveling into Steve's ear."

1. What's noise?
Noise produces vibrations that travel through the air as sound waves. When sound waves reach Steve's ears, they are gathered by the pinna (outer ear), which directs them into the auditory canal.

Fast growers
Steve's ears get bigger by about 0.08 in (2 mm) every nine years, which is ¼ in (6.35 mm) every 30 years. If Methuselah really had lived to be 969 years old (as the Bible reports), his ears would have been bigger than his head, and he could have used his earlobes as a hat!

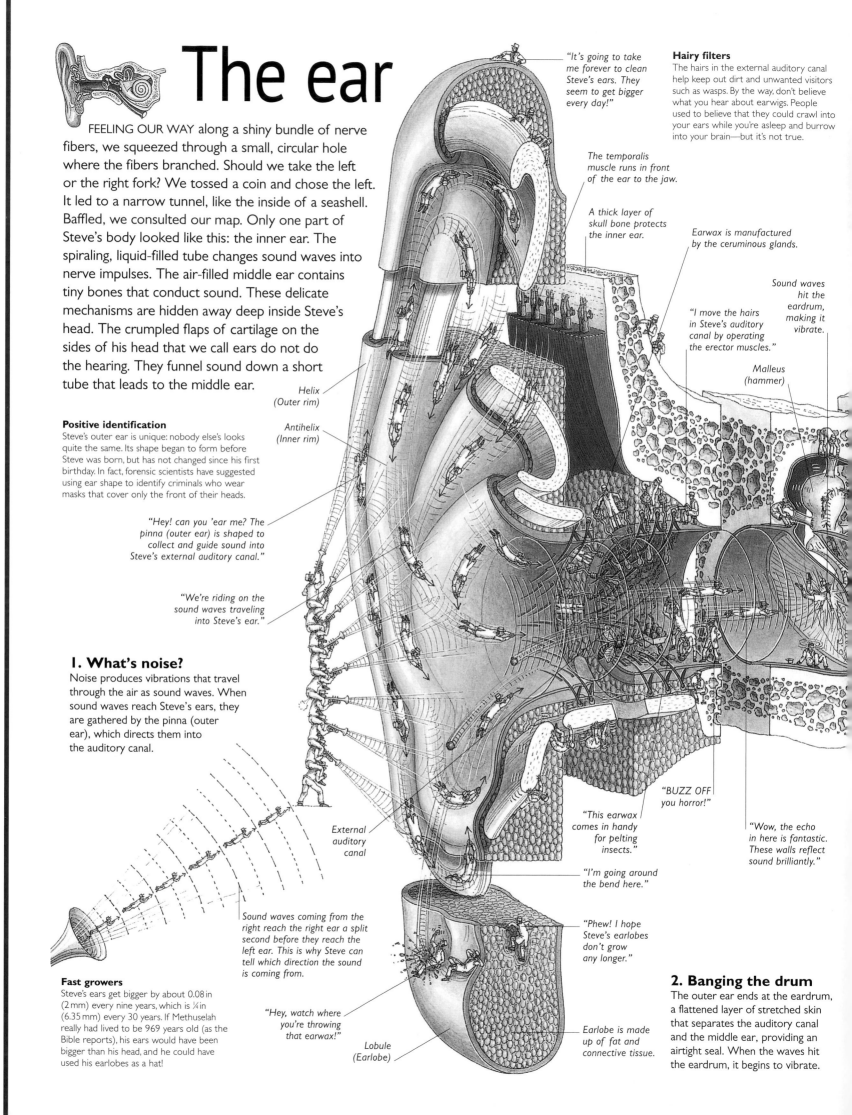

"It's going to take me forever to clean Steve's ears. They seem to get bigger every day!"

Hairy filters
The hairs in the external auditory canal help keep out dirt and unwanted visitors such as wasps. By the way, don't believe what you hear about earwigs. People used to believe that they could crawl into your ears while you're asleep and burrow into your brain—but it's not true.

The temporalis muscle runs in front of the ear to the jaw.

A thick layer of skull bone protects the inner ear.

Earwax is manufactured by the ceruminous glands.

Sound waves hit the eardrum, making it vibrate.

"I move the hairs in Steve's auditory canal by operating the erector muscles."

Malleus (hammer)

Helix (Outer rim)

Antihelix (Inner rim)

External auditory canal

Sound waves coming from the right reach the right ear a split second before they reach the left ear. This is why Steve can tell which direction the sound is coming from.

"Hey, watch where you're throwing that earwax!"

Lobule (Earlobe)

"This earwax comes in handy for pelting insects."

"I'm going around the bend here."

"Phew! I hope Steve's earlobes don't grow any longer."

Earlobe is made up of fat and connective tissue.

"BUZZ OFF you horror!"

"Wow, the echo in here is fantastic. These walls reflect sound brilliantly."

2. Banging the drum
The outer ear ends at the eardrum, a flattened layer of stretched skin that separates the auditory canal and the middle ear, providing an airtight seal. When the waves hit the eardrum, it begins to vibrate.

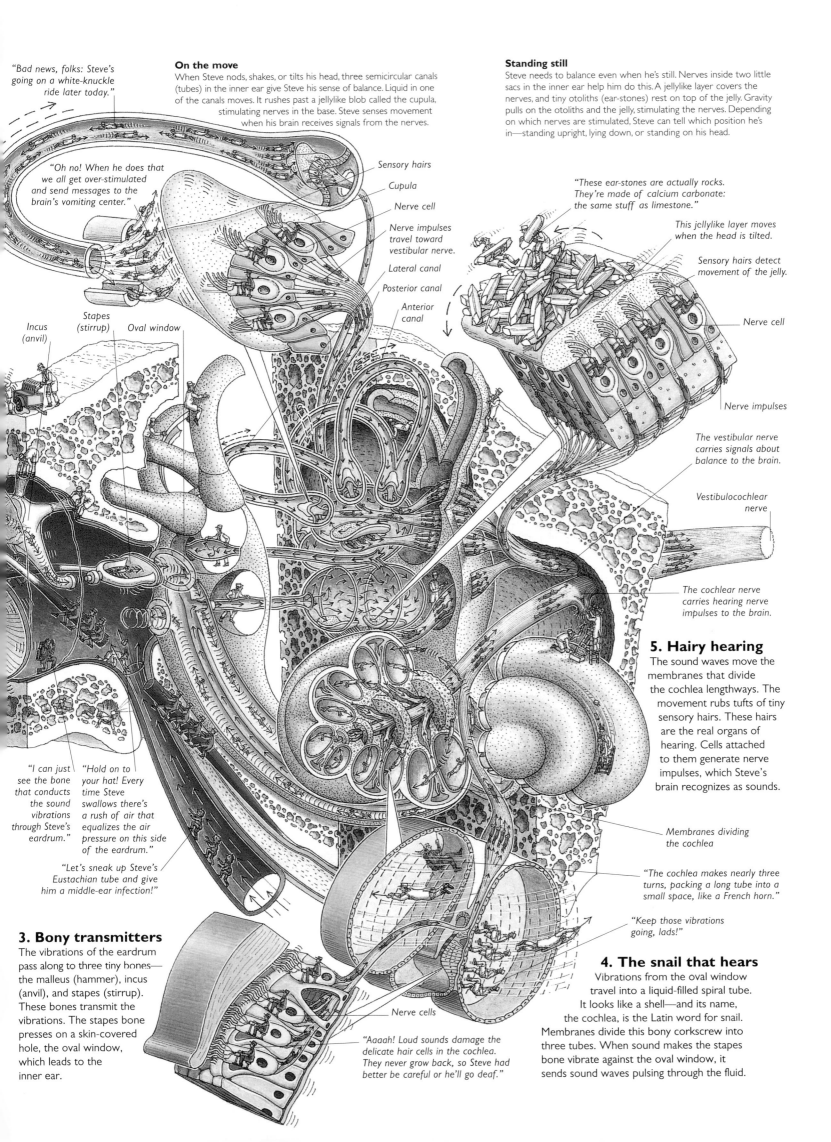

"Bad news, folks: Steve's going on a white-knuckle ride later today."

On the move
When Steve nods, shakes, or tilts his head, three semicircular canals (tubes) in the inner ear give Steve his sense of balance. Liquid in one of the canals moves. It rushes past a jellylike blob called the cupula, stimulating nerves in the base. Steve senses movement when his brain receives signals from the nerves.

Standing still
Steve needs to balance even when he's still. Nerves inside two little sacs in the inner ear help him do this. A jellylike layer covers the nerves, and tiny otoliths (ear-stones) rest on top of the jelly. Gravity pulls on the otoliths and the jelly, stimulating the nerves. Depending on which nerves are stimulated, Steve can tell which position he's in—standing upright, lying down, or standing on his head.

"Oh no! When he does that we all get over-stimulated and send messages to the brain's vomiting center."

Sensory hairs
Cupula
Nerve cell
Nerve impulses travel toward vestibular nerve.
Lateral canal
Posterior canal
Anterior canal

"These ear-stones are actually rocks. They're made of calcium carbonate: the same stuff as limestone."

This jellylike layer moves when the head is tilted.

Sensory hairs detect movement of the jelly.

Nerve cell

Nerve impulses

The vestibular nerve carries signals about balance to the brain.

Vestibulocochlear nerve

Incus (anvil)
Stapes (stirrup)
Oval window

The cochlear nerve carries hearing nerve impulses to the brain.

5. Hairy hearing
The sound waves move the membranes that divide the cochlea lengthways. The movement rubs tufts of tiny sensory hairs. These hairs are the real organs of hearing. Cells attached to them generate nerve impulses, which Steve's brain recognizes as sounds.

"I can just see the bone that conducts the sound vibrations through Steve's eardrum."

"Hold on to your hat! Every time Steve swallows there's a rush of air that equalizes the air pressure on this side of the eardrum."

"Let's sneak up Steve's Eustachian tube and give him a middle-ear infection!"

Membranes dividing the cochlea

"The cochlea makes nearly three turns, packing a long tube into a small space, like a French horn."

"Keep those vibrations going, lads!"

3. Bony transmitters
The vibrations of the eardrum pass along to three tiny bones—the malleus (hammer), incus (anvil), and stapes (stirrup). These bones transmit the vibrations. The stapes bone presses on a skin-covered hole, the oval window, which leads to the inner ear.

Nerve cells

"Aaaah! Loud sounds damage the delicate hair cells in the cochlea. They never grow back, so Steve had better be careful or he'll go deaf."

4. The snail that hears
Vibrations from the oval window travel into a liquid-filled spiral tube. It looks like a shell—and its name, the cochlea, is the Latin word for snail. Membranes divide this bony corkscrew into three tubes. When sound makes the stapes bone vibrate against the oval window, it sends sound waves pulsing through the fluid.

The brain

WE LEFT THE EAR AS WE HAD ENTERED: along a bundle of nerves. We chased a nervous impulse as it swooped inside Steve's skull and dived into his brainstem, but then lost it in the cerebellum. Searching would have been pointless: there are 100 billion nerve cells in a brain. Each is connected to thousands of neighbors, making the brain more complex than any computer. It needs to be. Steve's brain must carry out many tasks just to keep him alive. The brainstem keeps his heart beating and lungs breathing. The cerebrum, which makes up nine-tenths of the brain, enables him to think, and helps store memories. It also interprets nervous impulses from his senses and enables him to control his muscles. The brain is one of Steve's largest organs; it weighs around 3 lb (1.4 kg).

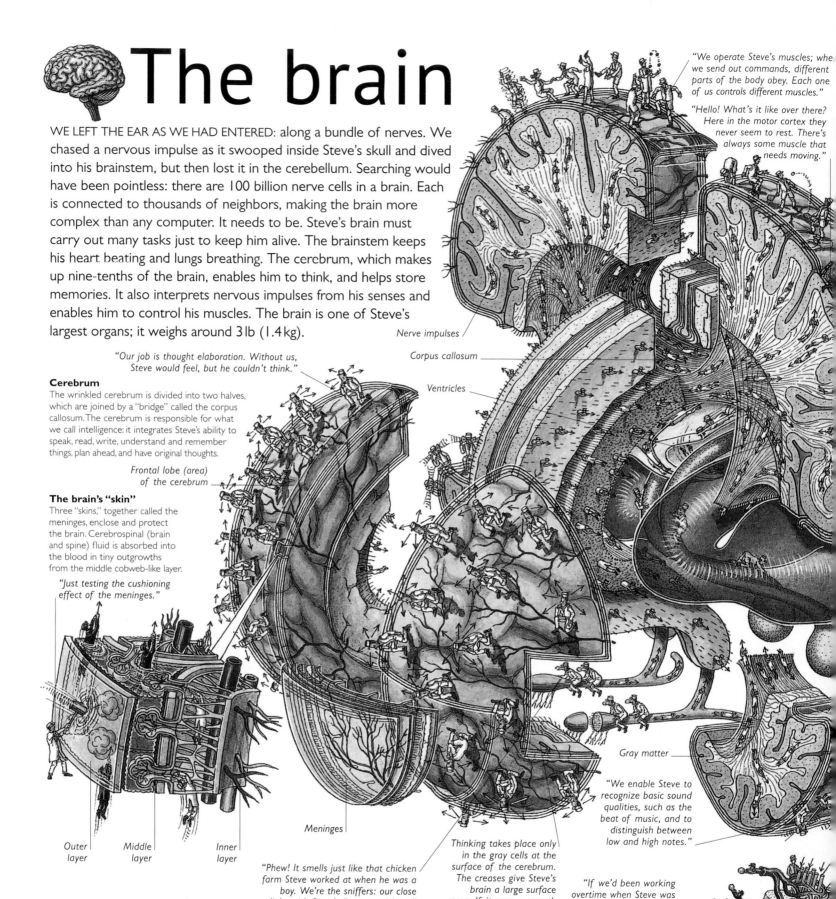

"We operate Steve's muscles; when we send out commands, different parts of the body obey. Each one of us controls different muscles."

"Hello! What's it like over there? Here in the motor cortex they never seem to rest. There's always some muscle that needs moving."

Nerve impulses

Corpus callosum

Ventricles

"Our job is thought elaboration. Without us, Steve would feel, but he couldn't think."

Cerebrum
The wrinkled cerebrum is divided into two halves, which are joined by a "bridge" called the corpus callosum. The cerebrum is responsible for what we call intelligence: it integrates Steve's ability to speak, read, write, understand and remember things, plan ahead, and have original thoughts.

Frontal lobe (area)
of the cerebrum

The brain's "skin"
Three "skins," together called the meninges, enclose and protect the brain. Cerebrospinal (brain and spine) fluid is absorbed into the blood in tiny outgrowths from the middle cobweb-like layer.

"Just testing the cushioning effect of the meninges."

Gray matter

"We enable Steve to recognize basic sound qualities, such as the beat of music, and to distinguish between low and high notes."

Outer layer | Middle layer | Inner layer

Meninges

"Phew! It smells just like that chicken farm Steve worked at when he was a boy. We're the sniffers: our close links with Steve's "emotional brain" (see top right) explains why smells bring back such vivid memories."

Thinking takes place only in the gray cells at the surface of the cerebrum. The creases give Steve's brain a large surface area. If it were a smooth ball, his head would need to be nearly twice as big for him to have the same intelligence.

"If we'd been working overtime when Steve was younger, we could have made him grow into an 8-ft (2.5-m) giant."

Left and right brain
The two sides of the cerebrum look very similar, and share much of the work of thinking. However, each side has special tasks. The left side enables Steve to figure out problems logically, speak and write, and understand science and numbers. The right side is his creative side. He gets his vivid imagination and artistic ability from here, as well as his appreciation of music.

The brain's inner room
Nerves carrying Steve's sensations converge on a region called the thalamus (inner chamber). The thalamus relays nervous impulses to the cerebrum, but can interpret sensation on its own: it helps Steve realize he is in pain, but other areas of the brain tell him where it hurts. The hypothalamus keeps Steve's autonomic nervous system working; it helps him control the movements of his heart, gut, and bladder, makes him hungry and thirsty, feel angry or aggressive, and stops him from falling asleep during the day.

Growth control
Like some other glands, the pituitary manufactures hormones—control chemicals distributed in the bloodstream. One of the functions of the pituitary gland is to control growth.

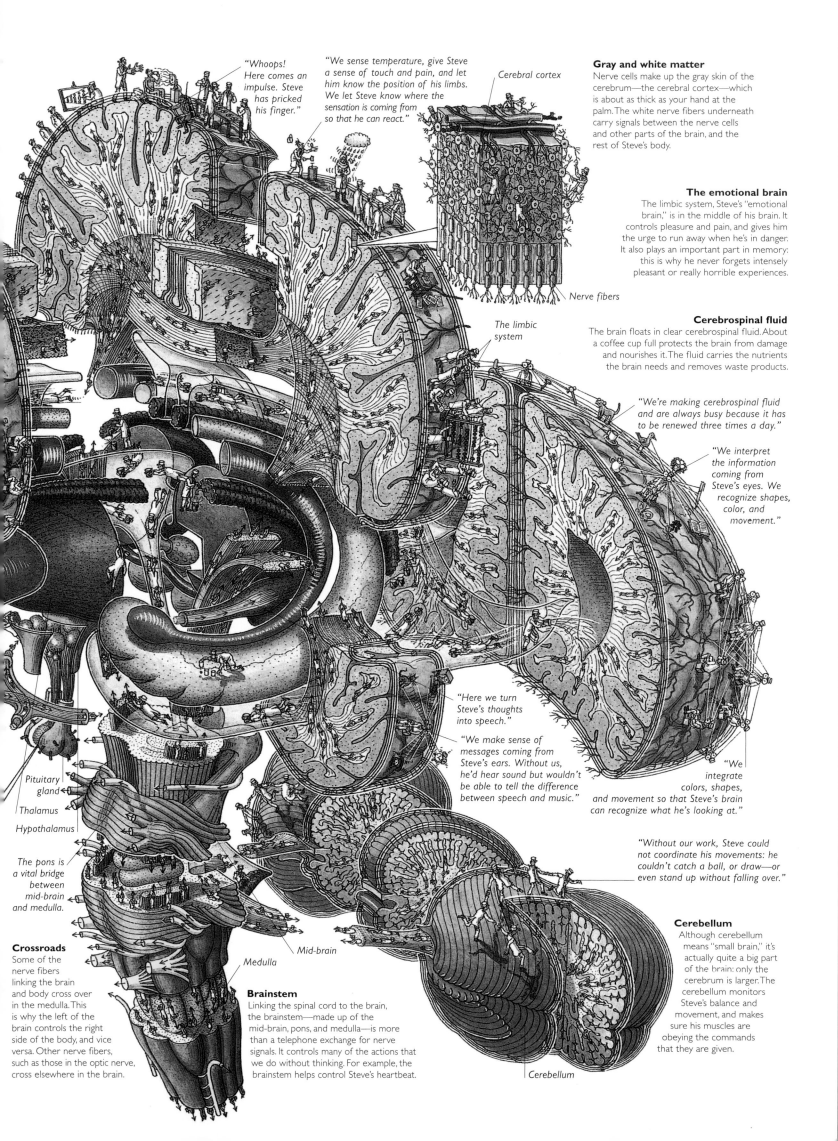

"Whoops! Here comes an impulse. Steve has pricked his finger."

"We sense temperature, give Steve a sense of touch and pain, and let him know the position of his limbs. We let Steve know where the sensation is coming from so that he can react."

Cerebral cortex

Gray and white matter

Nerve cells make up the gray skin of the cerebrum—the cerebral cortex—which is about as thick as your hand at the palm. The white nerve fibers underneath carry signals between the nerve cells and other parts of the brain, and the rest of Steve's body.

Nerve fibers

The emotional brain

The limbic system, Steve's "emotional brain," is in the middle of his brain. It controls pleasure and pain, and gives him the urge to run away when he's in danger. It also plays an important part in memory: this is why he never forgets intensely pleasant or really horrible experiences.

The limbic system

Cerebrospinal fluid

The brain floats in clear cerebrospinal fluid. About a coffee cup full protects the brain from damage and nourishes it. The fluid carries the nutrients the brain needs and removes waste products.

"We're making cerebrospinal fluid and are always busy because it has to be renewed three times a day."

"We interpret the information coming from Steve's eyes. We recognize shapes, color, and movement."

"Here we turn Steve's thoughts into speech."

"We make sense of messages coming from Steve's ears. Without us, he'd hear sound but wouldn't be able to tell the difference between speech and music."

"We integrate colors, shapes, and movement so that Steve's brain can recognize what he's looking at."

"Without our work, Steve could not coordinate his movements: he couldn't catch a ball, or draw—or even stand up without falling over."

Pituitary gland

Thalamus

Hypothalamus

The pons is a vital bridge between mid-brain and medulla.

Crossroads

Some of the nerve fibers linking the brain and body cross over in the medulla. This is why the left of the brain controls the right side of the body, and vice versa. Other nerve fibers, such as those in the optic nerve, cross elsewhere in the brain.

Mid-brain

Medulla

Brainstem

Linking the spinal cord to the brain, the brainstem—made up of the mid-brain, pons, and medulla—is more than a telephone exchange for nerve signals. It controls many of the actions that we do without thinking. For example, the brainstem helps control Steve's heartbeat.

Cerebellum

Although cerebellum means "small brain," it's actually quite a big part of the brain: only the cerebrum is larger. The cerebellum monitors Steve's balance and movement, and makes sure his muscles are obeying the commands that they are given.

Cerebellum

The spinal cord and nerves

AT THE BASE OF THE SKULL, a large hole led down into a tunnel. We slithered down it with great difficulty, as a shiny cable linked to the brain almost filled the tunnel's width. The cable was Steve's spinal cord, a thick bundle of nerve cells and fibers. The brain and spinal cord together form Steve's central nervous system. Nerve fibers spreading out from the spinal cord allow his brain and body to exchange information quickly. Sensory nerves carry messages up to Steve's brain (pp.12–13). They tell him he's hot or cold, where his limbs are, that he's pricked himself, his toe itches, or his bladder's full. Motor nerves carry the brain's instructions back down to his muscles and organs. Steve's spinal cord is delicate, and the slightest damage to it could cripple him. The cord is protected within his vertebrae—bony rings that together make up his spine.

"It's going to be a long day. We've got 66 ft (20 m) of spinal artery to repair and we've only done four."

1. Sense and response

Steve gathers information about the world around him using his senses—touch, sight, hearing, smell, and taste—and responds on the basis of this information.

2. Feeling pain

Touching a sharp object stimulates sensory nerves in the skin (pp.18–19). They send electrical messages (impulses) along nerves that run like wires up Steve's arm to his spine and up to his brain.

3. Ouch!

When rapid reaction is essential to avoid damage to the body, sensory impulses take a short cut, called a reflex action. Once inside the spinal cord, gray matter there identifies the nervous impulse as very urgent and sends the electrical messages two ways. One set of messages returns down the arm to lift the finger from the tack. The other goes to his brain to tell Steve he's in pain.

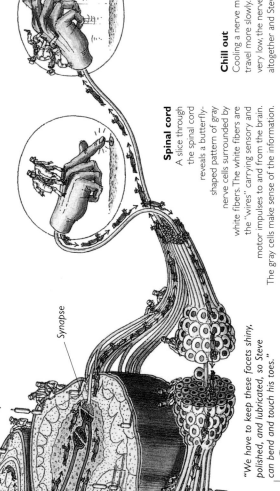

Spinal cord

A slice through the spinal cord reveals a butterfly-shaped pattern of gray nerve cells surrounded by white fibers. The white fibers are the "wires" carrying sensory and motor impulses to and from the brain. The gray cells make sense of the information.

Chill out

Cooling a nerve makes impulses in it travel more slowly. If the temperature is very low, the nerve may stop functioning altogether and Steve will feel numb.

Synapse

When Steve shakes his head to say "no," his skull rotates on a bony peg called the dens, which sticks up from the second neck vertebra.

Spinal cord

"We have to keep these facets shiny, polished, and lubricated, so Steve can bend and touch his toes."

Speeding spine

Nerve impulses can travel at great speeds: up to 430 ft (130 m) a second, as fast as a Formula I racing car. Nerve impulses go this fast only in thick nerve fibers that may be vital for survival. In thinner fibers they travel more slowly.

A relay race

Nerves communicate with each other, and with other tissues, at a junction called a synapse. When an electrical impulse reaches a synapse, it triggers the production of a chemical messenger called a neurotransmitter. The impulse passes the message to the neurotransmitter, which passes it on to the next nerve or muscle.

This nerve, carrying the pain signals from the finger of the left hand touching the tack, crosses to the right side of the spinal cord.

Impulses travel through axons in one direction only.

Axon

"How many skins has this thing got? It's just like an onion."

Nerve insulation

Axons (long nerve fibers) are wrapped in multiple layers of white fatty tissue. This coating works just like the plastic insulation of a wire: it prevents the tiny electrical signals from leaking out of the nerve, and speeds the nerve impulses along the axon.

This chain is made up of ganglia (bunches of nerve cells). It is called the sympathetic chain and controls involuntary actions, like the beating of Steve's heart.

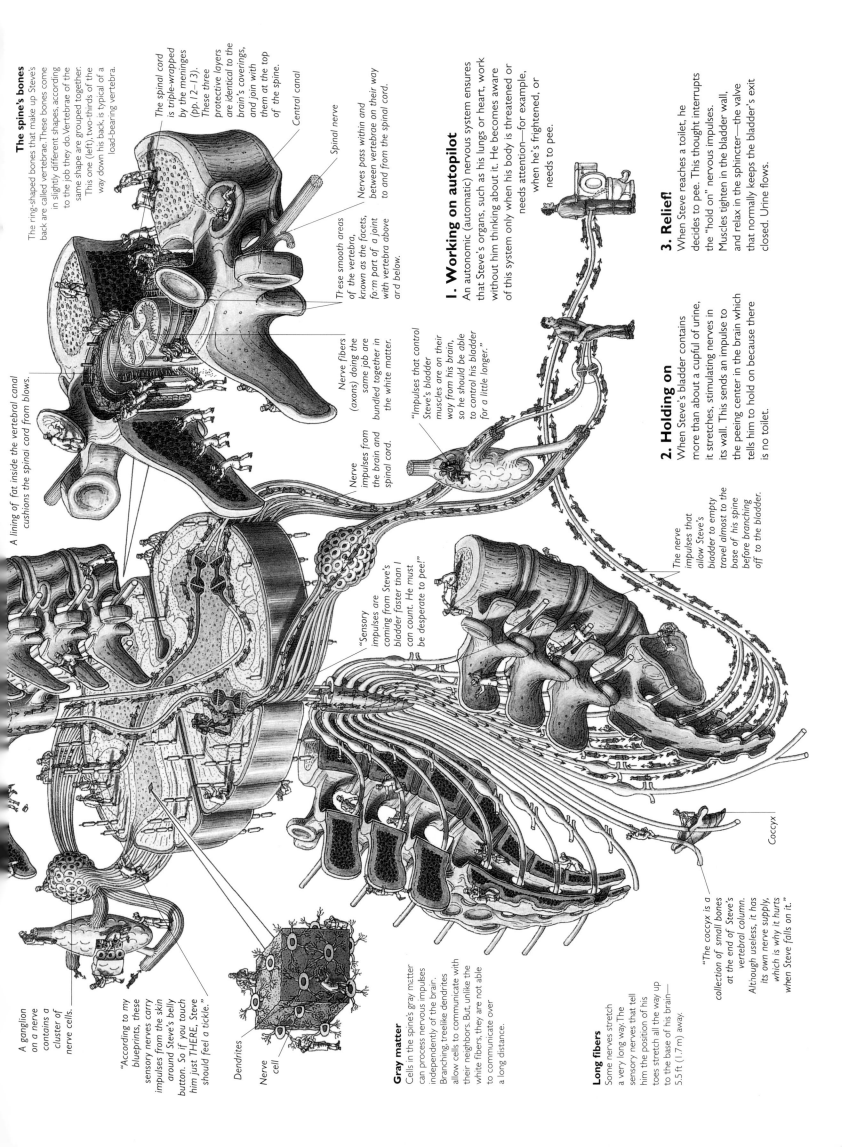

The spine's bones

The ring-shaped bones that make up Steve's back are called vertebrae. These bones come in slightly different shapes, according to the job they do. Vertebrae of the same shape are grouped together. This one (left), two-thirds of the way down his back, is typical of a load-bearing vertebra.

A lining of fat inside the vertebral canal cushions the spinal cord from blows.

The spinal cord is triple-wrapped by the meninges (pp.12–13). These three protective layers are identical to the brain's coverings, and join with them at the top of the spine.

Central canal

Spinal nerve

Nerves pass within and between vertebrae on their way to and from the spinal cord.

These smooth areas of the vertebra, known as the facets, form part of a joint with vertebra above and below.

Nerve fibers (axons) doing the same job are bundled together in the white matter.

Nerve impulses from the brain and spinal cord.

"Impulses that control Steve's bladder muscles are on their way from his brain, so he should be able to control his bladder for a little longer."

1. Working on autopilot

An autonomic (automatic) nervous system ensures that Steve's organs, such as his lungs or heart, work without him thinking about it. He becomes aware of this system only when his body is threatened or needs attention—for example, when he's frightened, or needs to pee.

2. Holding on

When Steve's bladder contains more than about a cupful of urine, it stretches, stimulating nerves in its wall. This sends an impulse to the peeing center in the brain which tells him to hold on because there is no toilet.

3. Relief!

When Steve reaches a toilet, he decides to pee. This thought interrupts the "hold on" nervous impulses. Muscles tighten in the bladder wall, and relax in the sphincter—the valve that normally keeps the bladder's exit closed. Urine flows.

The nerve impulses that allow Steve's bladder to empty travel almost to the base of his spine before branching off to the bladder.

Coccyx

"The coccyx is a collection of small bones at the end of Steve's vertebral column. Although useless, it has its own nerve supply, which is why it hurts when Steve falls on it."

"Sensory impulses are coming from Steve's bladder faster than I can count. He must be desperate to pee!"

A ganglion on a nerve contains a cluster of nerve cells.

"According to my blueprints, these sensory nerves carry impulses from the skin around Steve's belly button. So if you touch him just THERE, Steve should feel a tickle."

Gray matter

Cells in the spine's gray matter can process nervous impulses independently of the brain. Branching, treelike dendrites allow cells to communicate with their neighbors. But, unlike the white fibers, they are not able to communicate over a long distance.

Dendrites

Nerve cell

Long fibers

Some nerves stretch a very long way. The sensory nerves that tell him the position of his toes stretch all the way up to the base of his brain— 5.5 ft (1.7m) away.

The skeleton

ROPED TOGETHER FOR SAFETY, we climbed down from Steve's neck vertebrae into his rib cage. There we set up a base camp from which to investigate the rest of his bones. We were surprised by how fiendishly clever the skeleton is. You might think that the 206 bones of Steve's skeleton would weigh a lot, but the unique honeycomb structure of bone keeps it very light. Nevertheless bone is strong enough to support the weight of Steve's flesh and organs, and to protect vulnerable areas such as the brain. Bones are also a store of vital minerals, and the bone marrow inside them produces Steve's blood cells. Different sorts of joints allow the skeleton to twist and bend freely in the most vigorous of activities. When we had finished our study, we hitched a ride on a red blood cell, clinging on tight as it whirled away, carrying oxygen around Steve's body.

"It didn't break completely so it's called a greenstick fracture."

"It's healed up, because bone tissue is constantly renewed all over Steve's body."

Ribs

Narrow, curving bones called ribs support Steve's chest and protect the vital organs inside. Muscles attached to them help Steve breathe by expanding and contracting his chest cavity (pp.30–31). Steve has 12 pairs of ribs. All but the bottom two pairs are fixed to the backbone and, via strips of flexible cartilage, to the sternum. The bottom two pairs of "floating ribs" are attached only to the spine at the back.

The ribs are attached to the sternum by cartilage, allowing the rib cage to expand and contract.

The skull
The 22 bones of Steve's skull help give his face its unmistakable shape, and protect his brain from damage.

"These ear bones are the tiniest in Steve's body. But without them, Steve wouldn't hear a thing (pp.10–11)."

Tough teeth
Steve's teeth are made of dentine—a material similar to bone. The shiny coating of enamel on the visible part of his teeth is the hardest material in the human body, and the only one that is not exchanged or replaced as Steve gets older.

"These hollows in Steve's facial bones not only make his skull lighter, they also make his voice echo, giving it a distinctive sound."

Teeth remain intact long after the rest of the body has decomposed.

"Steve's jaw bone is the only moving part of his skull—and the muscles that move it are some of the strongest in his body."

"Look: Steve broke his collarbone here when he was younger."

Atlas

Axis

Pivot joint
A rotating joint at the top of Steve's spine allows him to turn his head left and right. A projection from the axis bone turns within a socket in the atlas bone.

Clavicle (collarbone)

Sternum (breastbone)

A ball and socket joint is the most flexible kind of joint in the body.

Ball and socket joint
This kind of joint allows for the greatest range of movement. A bony ball at the end of one bone fits inside a cup-shaped socket of another bone. In the shoulder joint, the rounded end of the humerus (upper arm) bone fits inside a socket in the scapula (shoulder blade), allowing Steve's arm to turn in many directions.

"Whee! The bones of Steve's arms and legs are the longest in his body."

Humerus (upper arm bone)

Scapula (shoulder blade)

Hinge joint
Steve's arm bends in the middle at the elbow. This joint is a hinge—like a door hinge, it opens and closes in one direction only.

"Steve gets shorter every day—and taller every night! Pressure from being upright squashes these rubbery disks while he's awake, making him lose half an inch or so in height between morning and evening. The disks expand again when he lies down."

Ulna

The radius and scaphoid bone of the hand meet in an ellipsoidal joint.

Saddle joint
These joints allow the bones to rock back and forth and from side to side.

Steve's bones are not dry at all inside—a quarter of their weight is water.

Radius

Powerful hands
The 27 bones in each of Steve's hands make them very flexible and useful. They allow him to hold a paintbrush delicately enough to create this extraordinary illustration. Yet, wrapped around a screwdriver, they can maintain enough force to drive in a screw.

Ilium (hip bone)

Ellipsoidal joint
At his wrist, Steve has an ellipsoidal joint. It allows him to move his hand left and right, and up and down.

"Let's pull Steve's knuckles apart until they crack! I just love that popping sound!"

Scaphoid

Trapezium

Floating rib

Bundles of stretchy fibers called ligaments join bones, giving strength and stability to a joint.

Metacarpal

Trapezium of wrist and first metacarpal of thumb fit together in a saddle joint.

"Steve's coccyx is useless, but a few vertebrae longer, and he'd have a tail to wag."

Coccyx

Bone structure
Compact bone tissue forms the outside layer of all bones, and the tubular shafts of long bones. It is the strongest form of bone because it's solid—there are few spaces between the hard cells. The spongy bone inside is like honeycomb. It's lighter than compact bone, but not as strong. The red bone marrow that fills the holes in spongy bone manufactures most of the cells of our blood.

Layers of cells and fibers run in different directions, giving bones extra strength.

Blood supply to the bone passes through tiny holes between cells.

Cartilage

Cartilage disks
Disks of springy material separate Steve's vertebrae. They give his spine flexibility, and allow it to absorb shock.

Free-moving joints
Without flexible connections between some of his bones, Steve could not move his body. Where they touch, the bones have a tough, shiny surface called cartilage that allows them to fit together easily. Synovial fluid keeps the joints moving smoothly, just as oil lubricates an engine.

"Look at this—the inside of Steve's long bones are lined with spongy bone."

Femur (thigh bone)

"A big joint like the knee contains nearly a teaspoonful of fluid."

Compact bone

Spongy bone

Bone marrow

Tibia (shinbone)

"I think I've figured out how we can hitch a ride out of here!"

The tarsals and metatarsals of the foot are joined by a gliding joint.

Fibula

Patella (kneecap)

Bone composition
Adult bones are two-thirds mineral and one-third bendy collagen. Bones are the body's biggest store of calcium. It is the calcium that makes them strong.

Gliding joint
A gliding joint is the simplest kind of free-moving joint in the body. In the foot, the small bones glide up and down only.

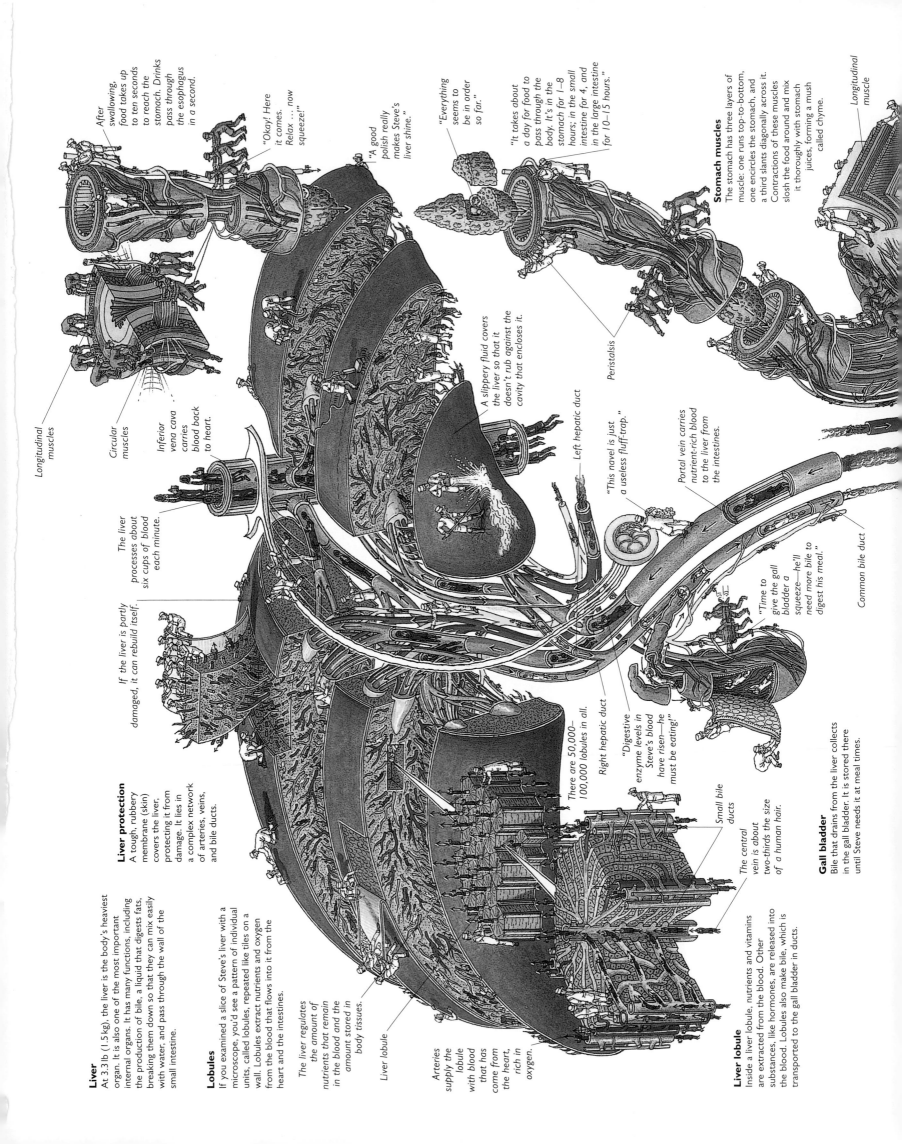

Liver

At 3.3lb (1.5kg), the liver is the body's heaviest organ. It is also one of the most important internal organs. It has many functions, including the production of bile, a liquid that digests fats, breaking them down so that they can mix easily with water, and pass through the wall of the small intestine.

Lobules

If you examined a slice of Steve's liver with a microscope, you'd see a pattern of individual units, called lobules, repeated like tiles on a wall. Lobules extract nutrients and oxygen from the blood that flows into it from the heart and the intestines.

Liver protection

A tough, rubbery membrane (skin) covers the liver, protecting it from damage. It lies in a complex network of arteries, veins, and bile ducts.

The liver regulates the amount of nutrients that remain in the blood and the amount stored in body tissues.

Arteries supply the lobule with blood that has come from the heart, rich in oxygen.

Liver lobule

Liver lobule

Inside a liver lobule, nutrients and vitamins are extracted from the blood. Other substances, like hormones, are released into the blood. Lobules also make bile, which is transported to the gall bladder in ducts.

The central vein is about two-thirds the size of a human hair.

Gall bladder

Bile that drains from the liver collects in the gall bladder. It is stored there until Steve needs it at meal times.

There are 50,000–100,000 lobules in all.

Small bile ducts

Right hepatic duct

"Digestive enzyme levels in Steve's blood have risen—he must be eating!"

"Time to give the gall bladder a squeeze—he'll need more bile to digest his meal."

Common bile duct

Portal vein carries nutrient-rich blood to the liver from the intestines.

"This novel is just a useless fluff-trap."

Left hepatic duct

A slippery fluid covers the liver so that it doesn't rub against the cavity that encloses it.

Peristalsis

If the liver is partly damaged, it can rebuild itself.

The liver processes about six cups of blood each minute.

Inferior vena cava carries blood back to heart.

Circular muscles

Longitudinal muscles

After swallowing, food takes up to ten seconds to reach the stomach. Drinks pass through the esophagus in a second.

"Okay! Here it comes. Relax ... now squeeze!"

"A good polish really makes Steve's liver shine."

"Everything seems to be in order so far."

"It takes about a day for food to pass through the body. It's in the stomach for 1–8 hours; in the small intestine for 4, and in the large intestine for 10–15 hours."

Stomach muscles

The stomach has three layers of muscle: one runs top-to-bottom, one encircles the stomach, and a third slants diagonally across it. Contractions of these muscles slosh the food around and mix it thoroughly with stomach juices, forming a mush called chyme.

Longitudinal muscle

The mouth and gut

AFTER STRUGGLING through the muscles that surround Steve's salivary glands, we emerged through a gumboil. We had hardly got our bearings before we were knocked over by a gigantic chip, then churned and chewed in a most terrifying manner. Thus began our journey through Steve's gut. This long tube begins at Steve's mouth and ends at his anus. When he eats, food is digested as it travels slowly through the gut. Digestion is the process of breaking down food into smaller bits so that the nutrients can be processed and absorbed. Parts of the gut do special jobs. The stomach, for instance, mixes food and breaks it up. The small intestine absorbs nutrients. Other organs, such as the liver and pancreas, aid digestion by supplying hormones and enzymes to dissolve and absorb food. And one organ, the appendix, is completely useless. It does nothing but cause trouble!

Tongue

Thousands of specially adapted cells in Steve's mouth allow him to taste what he eats. Most of the cells are on his tongue. Steve's taste detectors are called taste buds. They line tiny folds that surround small swellings on the surface of his tongue. Saliva carries dissolved food into the folds, stimulating the taste buds.

The mushroom-shaped swellings are found mostly on the tip and sides of the tongue.

Taste buds

Most of the taste buds lie beneath the tongue's deeply folded surface. Receptor cells that detect flavor line the inside of the bud. Only their hairlike tips protrude through a pore (tiny hole).

Saliva

Taste bud

Sensations of taste travel along nerve fibers to the limbic system of the brain.

Receptor cell

"Steve's going down to the Khyber Pass Curry House tonight."

Flavors enter in saliva through a taste pore.

Taste hairs

"What! Better order up some reserves. These cells won't last an hour if he has the Chicken Vindaloo Extra Hot again."

Taste information going to the brain

The salivary glands under the jaw bone add mucus to saliva, making Steve's spit sticky.

Mouth

Steve's teeth tear up food into small pieces, and his tongue pushes them back to his throat so that he can swallow them.

Salivary glands

Special glands in front of Steve's ears and under his tongue produce saliva. This watery liquid wets the mouth and starts to digest food into a sticky mass that Steve can swallow.

"Quickly team, we've had an order from the brainstem (pp. 12–13). Apparently Steve has sniffed a delicious chip, and we've got to make his mouth water. So get going on the saliva pumps."

Pharynx (throat)

Chewed-up food reaches the throat from the mouth and is then swallowed automatically. The tough fleshy flap of the epiglottis closes off the windpipe until the food is safely on its way to his stomach.

"Another big pull now: we don't want these chips to go down the wrong way."

Esophagus

This muscular tube carries food from Steve's mouth to his stomach. When chewed-up food enters at the top, rings of layered muscles contract, squeezing the food downward.

Shiny, outer layer

Longitudinal muscle

Circular muscle

Layers protect the esophagus from hot or spicy food.

Thyroid gland

The thyroid gland in Steve's neck manufactures vital hormones that control his metabolic rate—the speed at which energy provided by food gets used up. If Steve's thyroid gland didn't work he would become overweight.

Peristalsis

To move food along, the muscular walls of the esophagus squeeze and relax in carefully coordinated waves called peristalsis.

Skin and muscles

WHEN THE RED BLOOD CELL we were riding slowed down we jumped off, landing under the skin of Steve's chin. Besides protecting his body, this supple leathery layer keeps him cool, gives him a sense of touch, and even makes vitamins! But after a close shave with a razor blade we decided to retreat to somewhere safer. We snuggled down into a facial muscle, planning to rest, but it was hopeless. It turned out that the muscle was attached to the corners of Steve's mouth, and he was laughing at his own jokes! Giving up hope of sleep, we split up and explored other parts of Steve's skin and muscles.

Muscles and movement
To move his body, Steve uses muscles—bundles of fleshy tissue fixed to his bones. Each muscle is made of small fibers that contract (get shorter) or relax (lengthen) when a nerve signal reaches them. By shortening or lengthening, the muscles may cause bones to move, or lips to smile.

Frowning muscles
Steve may use nine muscles when he frowns—to furrow his brow, narrow his eyes, widen his nostrils, and pull down the corners of his mouth.

Furrowing the brow

Narrowing the eye

Flaring the nostrils

Muscle tone
When Steve lies down to rest, his muscles relax and his body goes limp. But even at rest, muscles never relax completely; a few fibers are always contracting, giving muscles a firmness called tone.

Pricking the skin and injecting dye beneath it makes a permanent mark called a tattoo.

Fingerprints
The patterns of ridges and furrows on the skin of Steve's hands are unique—nobody else leaves fingerprints that are quite the same as his.

Biceps

"Come and look at these tendons—his hand's like a rope factory."

The muscles running outside the rib cage help Steve breathe.

"There she blows! This disgusting pus is caused by oil blocking a hair follicle, making it infected. We call it a zit."

Nail

Nail structure
The nails on Steve's fingers and toes are made of cells rich in a tough protein called keratin. Nails grow from special cells hidden under the cuticle.

Cuticle

If Steve tried all the muscles out in different combinations, he could pull 7,000 different faces.

Muscle structure
Muscles are made like bundles of bundles of bundles. Look closely at one and you'll see it's made of many tiny fibers, all aligned the same way. With a microscope, you could see that each fiber is also a bundle of even smaller threads. These threads are themselves bundles of even smaller threads called fibrils.

The sartorius muscle that crosses the thigh is the longest muscle in Steve's body.

Ligaments are stretchy enough to allow free movement, yet tough enough to stand up to powerful pulling forces.

Muscle filaments
The smallest fibrils are so tiny that if a human hair were a tube, 150 million fibrils would fit inside. They give the muscle its pulling ability. When a nervous impulse from the brain reaches them (pp.12–13), filaments inside the fibrils slide past each other, making the muscle contract.

Ligaments
Actions such as running put great stress on Steve's joints. Ligaments stop his bones from flying apart. These bands of rubbery tissue are fixed to the bones close to where they meet at each joint (pp.16–17).

Fiber

The largest muscle fibers are as thick as a human hair, and the smallest are a tenth as thick.

Fibrils

Pulling down the corners of the mouth

Smiling muscles
A big, hearty grin may use eight muscles—to pull up the brow, to widen the eyes, to raise the upper lip, and to pull up the corners of the mouth.

Pulling up the brow

Head hair
Steve's scalp is similar to skin elsewhere on his body. The main difference is that the hairs on his head grow longer, coarser, and faster than the fine hairs that cover the skin on the rest of his body.

"Looking after these hairs is a breeze. My last job was on a sheep, and its fleece grew three times as fast."

Hair
The hair that's visible above Steve's scalp is completely dead. It's mostly made of keratin. Hairs are alive only at the root, where growth takes place.

Tiny, hard scales cover a softer, flexible core.

Muscles at work
During activity, Steve contracts (shortens) some of his muscles and relaxes others. To ensure that every part of Steve's body can move back as well as forward, each muscle has another one opposing (working against) it. For example, the biceps bends the arm at the elbow. The triceps straightens it.

Skin contains pigment to protect it from the damaging effects of sunlight. Sunlight speeds up pigment production, which is why skin tans.

Triceps

Deltoid

Widening the eyes

The skin of Steve's eyelids is thinner than anywhere else.

Pulling the mouth up

Raising the upper lip

Lifting the corner of the mouth

Bacteria multiply on the skin in the warm, sweaty conditions of the armpit and create a smell.

Protective skin
All that separates Steve from the world around him is 22 square feet (2 m²) of skin. Besides keeping his body in, skin also keeps water, dirt, and microbes out, and helps regulate his body temperature.

Epidermis

When Steve plays squash for seven minutes, his muscles produce enough heat to boil water for four cups of tea.

Oil glands produce a waxy goo that helps waterproof the skin.

Tendons are so tough and elastic that those of animals were once used to strengthen archery bows.

Steve's skin flakes off constantly and is continually replaced.

"No, YOU come HERE! I'm busy with the plumbing in Steve's skin."

Achilles tendon

Dermis

Muscles in his tongue contract when he sticks it out.

Many different kinds of nerves lie just beneath the skin's surface. They allow Steve to detect heat, cold, pressure, touch, vibration, tickle, and pain (pp.14–15).

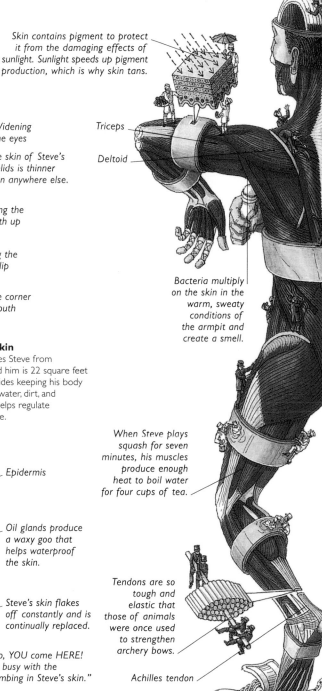

Dermis
Beneath the epidermis is a tough, stretchy layer containing blood vessels, nerves, and hair follicles. This layer is thin over Steve's joints where it has to be especially flexible, and is thickest on his palms and soles. New skin cells are manufactured here and migrate through the epidermis, where they are eventually shed.

Epidermis
The outer layer of Steve's skin is about as thick as a piece of good-quality writing paper. Nine-tenths of its cells manufacture keratin. Keratin collects on the skin surface, making it waterproof, and protecting the layers below. Most of the remaining cells produce pigment or help protect Steve from infection.

Tendons
Muscles aren't always attached directly to the bones they move. Sometimes a tough tissue called a tendon links the bone to a distant muscle. The tendon acts like a rope: muscular contractions pull the tendon, and the tendon in turn pulls the bone.

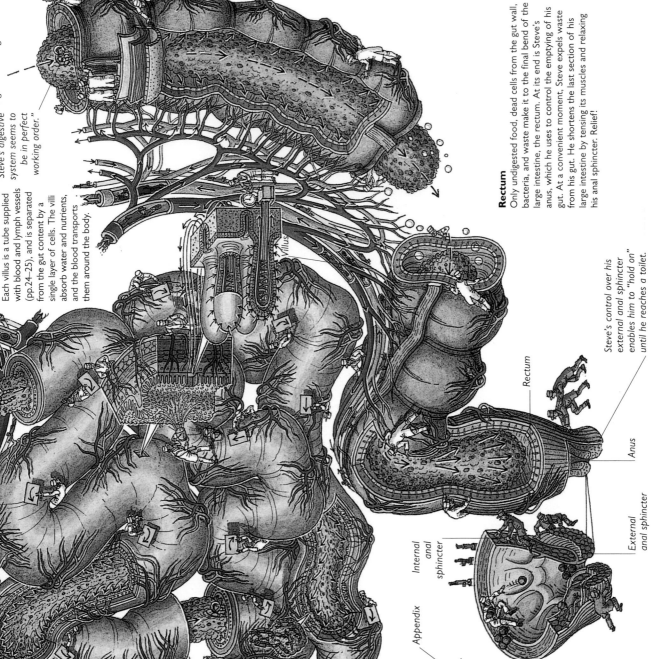

Breaking wind

Digestion produces gases that cause discomfort unless they are expelled from the gut. Most people do this about 13 times a day. Some of the gases that make up flatus—hydrogen sulfide, hydrogen, and methane—are explosive. They also contribute to global warming!

"Steve's digestive system seems to be in perfect working order."

Villi

The gut wall is lined with hairlike fingers called villi. Each villus is a tube supplied with blood and lymph vessels (pp.24–25), and is separated from the gut content by a single layer of cells. The villi absorb water and nutrients, and the blood transports them around the body.

Villus

Rectum

Only undigested food, dead cells from the gut wall, bacteria, and waste make it to the final bend of the large intestine, the rectum. At its end is Steve's anus, which he uses to control the emptying of his gut. At a convenient moment, Steve expels waste from his gut. He shortens the last section of his large intestine by tensing its muscles and relaxing his anal sphincter. Relief!

Rectum

Anus

Steve's control over his external anal sphincter enables him to "hold on" until he reaches a toilet.

External anal sphincter

Internal anal sphincter

Pancreatic tissue

The tissue of the pancreas involves clusters called islets of Langerhans. The special cells in these clusters produce two hormones which flow not into the gut, but into the blood. The hormones—insulin and glucagon—work together to control and regulate the level of glucose (sugar) in the blood. Glucose is the main fuel of the cells in Steve's body.

Wiggly wall

The small intestine's maze-like path crams a very long tube into a compact space. And because the inside of the gut is deeply folded, it has a huge surface through which nutrients and water can be absorbed. The surface area of the small intestine is 350 square yards (290 m²). This is 200 times the area of Steve's skin, and slightly more than the area of a tennis court.

An adult's small intestine is about 21 ft (6.5 m) long: enough to make casings for 40–50 sausages.

The large intestine

The final stages of digestion take place in the large intestine, which loops up, across, and down Steve's body like a horseshoe. Here bacteria help break down what's left of the food. The walls of the large intestine allow water and nutrients to pass through; all that leaves the large intestine is waste.

Roughly a bucket of liquid flows through our guts each day. Most liquids are the body's own secretions and all but half a cup of the liquid is reabsorbed through the gut wall into blood and lymph.

Appendix

At the beginning of the large intestine, the appendix is the joke organ of the gut. It's a small tube, the shape and size of Steve's middle finger, and it does very little other than get blocked occasionally.

Appendix

"If Steve's appendix doesn't stop grumbling, we may have to chop it off to prevent infection spreading."

Anal sphincters

Steve's anus is kept tightly closed by not one, but two sphincters (valves). The anal sphincters are under the control of Steve's nervous system (pp.14–15) and open whenever pressure increases in the gut.

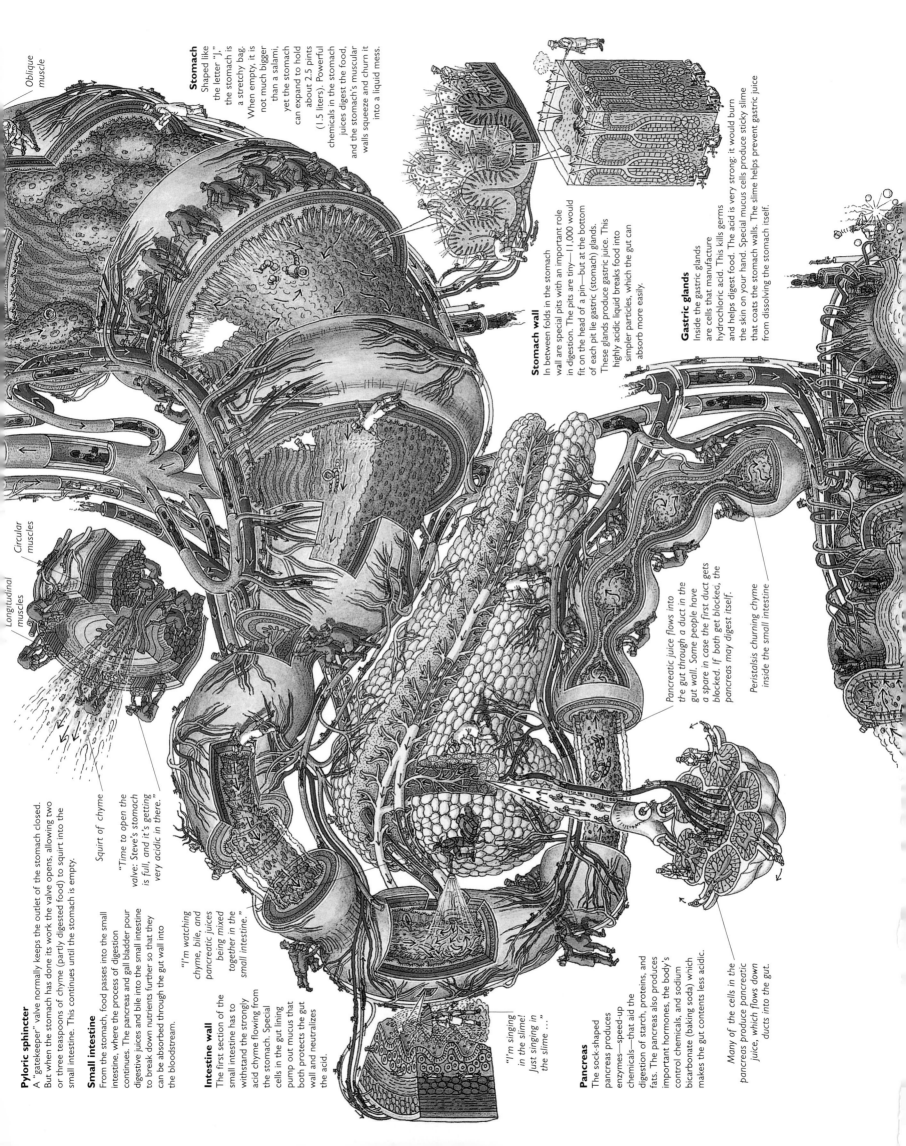

Oblique muscle

Stomach

Shaped like the letter "J," the stomach is a stretchy bag. When empty, it is not much bigger than a salami, yet the stomach can expand to hold about 2.5 pints (1.5 liters). Powerful chemicals in the stomach juices digest the food, and the stomach's muscular walls squeeze and churn it into a liquid mess.

Stomach wall

In between folds in the stomach wall are special pits with an important role in digestion. The pits are tiny—11,000 would fit on the head of a pin—but at the bottom of each pit lie gastric (stomach) glands. These glands produce gastric juice. This highly acidic liquid breaks food into simpler particles, which the gut can absorb more easily.

Gastric glands

Inside the gastric glands are cells that manufacture hydrochloric acid. This kills germs and helps digest food. The acid is very strong: it would burn the skin on your hand. Special mucus cells produce sticky slime that coats the stomach walls. The slime helps prevent gastric juice from dissolving the stomach itself.

Circular muscles

Longitudinal muscles

Pancreatic juice flows into the gut through a duct in the gut wall. Some people have a spare in case the first duct gets blocked. If both get blocked, the pancreas may digest itself.

Peristalsis churning chyme inside the small intestine

Pyloric sphincter

A "gatekeeper" valve normally keeps the outlet of the stomach closed. But when the stomach has done its work the valve opens, allowing two or three teaspoons of chyme (partly digested food) to squirt into the small intestine. This continues until the stomach is empty.

Squirt of chyme

Small intestine

From the stomach, food passes into the small intestine, where the process of digestion continues. The pancreas and gall bladder pour digestive juices and bile into the small intestine to break down nutrients further so that they can be absorbed through the gut wall into the bloodstream.

"Time to open the valve: Steve's stomach is full, and it's getting very acidic in there."

"I'm watching chyme, bile, and pancreatic juices being mixed together in the small intestine."

Intestine wall

The first section of the small intestine has to withstand the strongly acid chyme flowing from the stomach. Special cells in the gut lining pump out mucus that both protects the gut wall and neutralizes the acid.

"I'm singing in the slime! Just singing in the slime ..."

Pancreas

The sock-shaped pancreas produces enzymes—speed-up chemicals—that aid the digestion of starch, proteins, and fats. The pancreas also produces important hormones, the body's control chemicals, and sodium bicarbonate (baking soda) which makes the gut contents less acidic.

Many of the cells in the pancreas produce pancreatic juice, which flows down ducts into the gut.

Lymph and blood

I THOUGHT WE'D EXPLORED EVERY TUBE in Steve's body, but I was wrong. We hitched a ride on a sugar molecule in Steve's blood. As it took us through a particularly narrow channel, we were swept into a completely new network of tubes. They were filled with a clear liquid called lymph. An army of white cells swarmed around us. They protect Steve against infection (germ attack). Blood carries them around the body. It moves the white cells from their own special network of lymph tissue to where germs threaten. Germs attack through wounds and through Steve's mouth and nose. White cells remember every germ they fight and its weaknesses. (This way they can fight a germ more quickly if it makes a second attack.)

To understand how effective they are, think of a piece of meat left out on a hot day—it decays rapidly. Steve's whole body would rot just as quickly if not for the work of his white cells.

Spleen
The biggest collection of lymphatic tissue in Steve's body is the spleen, which nestles just behind Steve's stomach. Unlike lymph nodes, the spleen does not filter the lymph that flows through it. Instead, cells in the white pulp there eat up bacteria.

Red pulp
Spongy red tissue in the spleen filters large amounts of blood. If an injury cuts through one of Steve's arteries, the spleen can make extra red blood cells to make up for the blood Steve loses through the wound.

"Come and look at Steve's spleen: it's just like a sponge. At any one time nearly a fifth of his blood is being filtered in here."

"Get a move on lads. We've got to sweep up two million dead red cells each SECOND!"

Germ warfare
Steve would be very ill if germs spread around his body, so he has many ways to prevent infection. Some are general defenses that give him resistance against all germs. Others target one germ only. Both types leap into action if Steve cuts his knee.

Thymus gland
Sandwiched between Steve's windpipe and his chest wall is the thymus gland. This is where T-cells mature.

The thymus gland is named after its shape—it resembles the leaf of a thyme plant.

"GULP! Yum, I just can't get enough of these dead red cells!"

Spleen

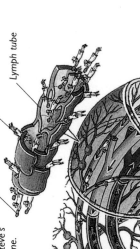

Adenoids
To protect himself against germs he breathes in, Steve has a big cluster of lymph tissue at the back of his nose.

"Everyone calls them adenoids, but they're actually more tonsils."

"Move out these T-cells—they've been here a week, so they're grown up enough to go and fight germs by now."

Thymus gland

Powerful plumbing
Steve's bloodstream transports white cells wherever they are needed. Arteries, a network of pipes, carry blood from Steve's heart (pp.28–29) to his tissues. Blood flows back to the heart along pipes called veins. Tiny tubes called capillaries connect the veins and arteries. All these pipes and tubes are called blood vessels.

Lymph tubes of upper arm

Lymph tubes of lower arm

Lymph
This clear fluid moves white blood cells within the lymph tubes. Lymph also collects proteins from the tissues and adjusts the flow of the tissue fluid that bathes Steve's cells. In fact, lymph and tissue fluid are the same liquid. Tissue fluid is called lymph as soon as it enters a lymph tube.

Tonsils
Right at the back of Steve's mouth, this large cluster of lymph tissue guards Steve against germs he eats or drinks. If germs infect Steve's tonsils, they swell and turn red.

Salivary gland

"We do a vital job guarding against germs. The mouth and nose are their main route into Steve's body."

Lymph merges with the bloodstream just below Steve's collarbone.

Tonsils

Tear glands

Lymph tubes
A network of tiny tubes keeps lymph on the move. There's no central pump, like the heart, to squirt lymph along. Instead lymph flows when Steve's muscles contract, squeezing the tubes that carry it. Valves make sure the lymph moves one way only.

Lymph nodes
Spaced at intervals along the tubes, lymph nodes filter the lymph. As lymph flows through a node, the white blood cells in it identify and destroy anything that could harm Steve's body. There are several kinds of white blood cells: scavenger cells eat germs, T-cells and B-cells identify and kill germs.

"We will splash into a bigger lymph tube soon."

Fluid in the surrounding tissues seeps into the lymph tube through holes in the tube's walls.

Lymph tube

Oxygenated blood from lungs

"Pump faster! We need to send lots of white cells to defend Steve's knee."

Brachial artery

Spleen

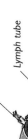

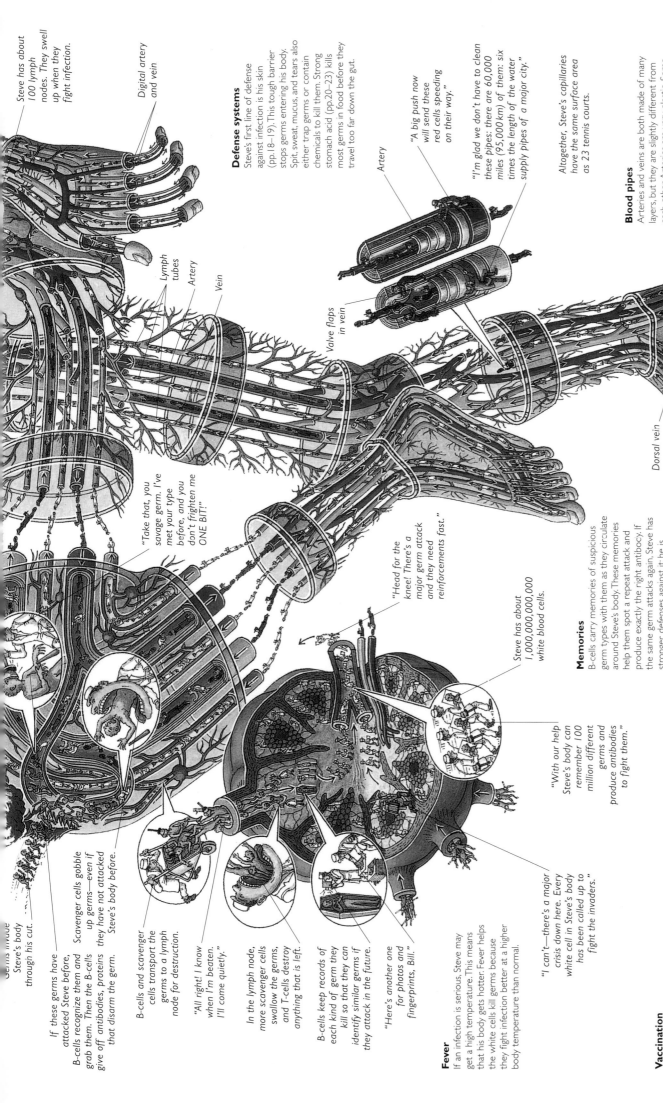

Steve has about 100 lymph nodes. They swell up when they fight infection.

Digital artery and vein

Defense systems
Steve's first line of defense against infection is his skin (pp.18–19). This tough barrier stops germs entering his body. Spit, sweat, mucus, and tears also either trap germs or contain chemicals to kill them. Strong stomach acid (pp.20–23) kills most germs in food before they travel too far down the gut.

Artery

"A big push now will send these red cells speeding on their way."

"I'm glad we don't have to clean these pipes: there are 60,000 miles (95,000 km) of them: six times the length of the water supply pipes of a major city."

Altogether, Steve's capillaries have the same surface area as 23 tennis courts.

Blood pipes
Arteries and veins are both made of many layers, but they are slightly different from each other. Arteries are very elastic. Some widen as each heartbeat sends out a pulse of blood. Blood flows through veins at a lower pressure, so the walls of veins are thinner. One-way valves in veins keep the blood flowing toward the heart.

Lymph tubes

Artery

Vein

Valve flaps in vein

Dorsal artery

Dorsal vein

Digital artery and vein

"Take that, you savage germ. I've met your type before, and you don't frighten me ONE BIT!"

"Head for the knee! There's a major germ attack and they need reinforcements fast."

Steve has about 1,000,000,000 white blood cells.

Memories
B-cells carry memories of suspicious germ types with them as they circulate around Steve's body. These memories help them spot a repeat attack and produce exactly the right antibody. If the same germ attacks again, Steve has stronger defenses against it: he is immune to that germ.

Germs invade Steve's body through his cut.

If these germs have attacked Steve before, B-cells recognize them and grab them. Then the B-cells give off antibodies, proteins that disarm the germ.

Scavenger cells gobble up germs—even if they have not attacked Steve's body before.

B-cells and scavenger cells transport the germs to a lymph node for destruction.

"All right! I know when I'm beaten. I'll come quietly."

In the lymph node, more scavenger cells swallow the germs, and T-cells destroy anything that is left.

B-cells keep records of each kind of germ they kill so that they can identify similar germs if they attack in the future.

"Here's another one for photos and fingerprints, Bill."

"I can't—there's a major crisis down here. Every white cell in Steve's body has been called up to fight the invaders."

"With our help Steve's body can remember 100 million different germs and produce antibodies to fight them."

Inflammation
Steve's tissues respond to damage by becoming inflamed. Blood flows more quickly than usual in the area around the cut, carrying plenty of healing white cells to combat infection. The extra blood makes the cut swell, redden, and get hot (inflammation).

Fever
If an infection is serious, Steve may get a high temperature. This means that his body gets hotter. Fever helps the white cells kill germs because they fight infection better at a higher body temperature than normal.

Vaccination
Through vaccination, Steve is immune to diseases he's never caught. For example, when Steve was vaccinated against polio, his doctor gave him a dose of polio virus that had been chemically killed or weakened. Steve did not catch the disease, but the vaccination enables his body to produce the correct antibodies that will protect him if he's ever exposed to live polio virus.

The kidneys, bladder, and reproductive system

THE QUICKEST WAY TO EXPLORE STEVE'S BODY must be on the back of a water molecule. They're 20,000 times smaller than red blood cells, so they move around much faster. When we reached a kidney, though, our choice of transport sent us skidding out of the blood-stream. Red cells floated on, but we slipped out of the vein through a tiny hole, and ended up swimming in urine! Steve's two kidneys filter his blood. They remove poisons and excess water, and the waste collects in his bladder as urine. Steve empties his bladder through his penis. Steve's penis also does another job. It acts as a pipeline for sperm (male seed cells) during reproduction.

"Why are we bothering with repairs? If one of Steve's kidneys failed, he could manage with just the other one."

Kidneys on show

Steve's two bean-shaped kidneys nestle inside his rib cage on either side of his spine, just above his waist. Large arteries and veins carry blood to and from the kidneys. Urine that collects in the kidneys' hollow centers drains away to the bladder along tubes called ureters (urine ducts).

Kidney anatomy

Blood enters a kidney at its center and flows through branching arteries to the outside edge. There 30 million tiny filtration units purify the blood.

"These kidneys are amazingly efficient: they clean and filter all of Steve's blood every 25 minutes."

Layers of fat and tough tissue enclose each kidney to protect it from damage.

"This fatty covering protects the kidney against all but the hardest knocks."

Urine ducts

At their thickest, Steve's ureters (urine ducts) are still thinner than his little finger. Each has muscular walls that can squeeze the tube inside, forcing urine down toward the bladder.

Blood filtration units

In the kidneys, blood flows through narrow vessels lining tiny bulbs, which act like sieves. Water, salts, and some sugars pass out of the blood, collecting as fluid in the bulbs. This fluid flows along looping tubes, where most of the water returns to the bloodstream, along with valuable salts. Waste products continue to filter out of the blood and into the fluid, which becomes urine.

The looping tubes in Steve's kidneys keep the acidity of Steve's blood constant.

To help filtration, the walls of the blood vessels are 150 times thinner than a piece of writing paper.

"I'm going to dive in now and swim toward you, but which way should I go?"

Cortex

Medulla

Channeling urine

Urine flows into a cone-shaped area of tissue filled with tiny channels. These merge into larger ducts, channeling urine into a collecting chamber at the kidney's center.

Adrenal gland

On the top of each kidney, these glands manufacture hormones—vital controlling chemicals that travel around the body in the bloodstream (pp.24–25). One of them, adrenaline, is released when Steve is in danger.

"The holes in these filters are really tiny: a grain of sand would be 10,000 times too big to pass through them."

"The adrenaline we pump into Steve's blood gives him instant energy and makes him want to fight, or run for safety."

Renal artery

Renal vein

Adrenal gland

Bladder

Urine flowing from Steve's kidneys is stored in his bladder. This muscular bag is big enough to hold about three cups of urine. The bladder's elastic walls stretch as it fills, but the stretching stimulates nerves. These warn Steve to look for a lavatory (pp.14–15).

Bladder

Ureter (urine duct)

Ureter (urine duct)

Iliac vein

Iliac artery

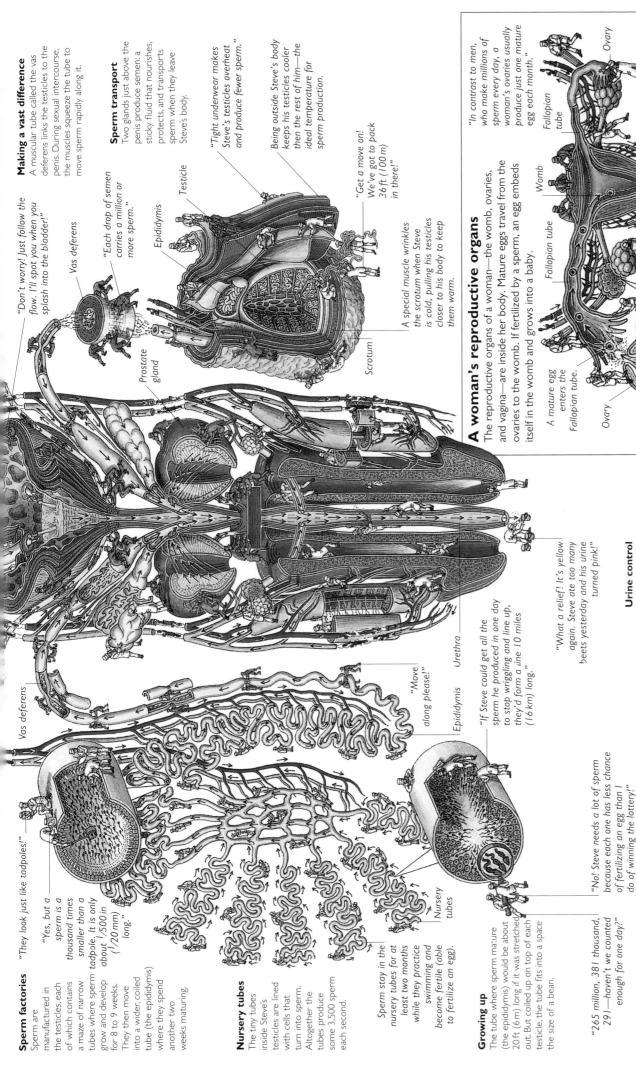

Sperm factories

Sperm are manufactured in the testicles, each of which contains a maze of narrow tubes where sperm grow and develop for 8 to 9 weeks. They then move into a wider, coiled tube (the epididymis) where they spend another two weeks maturing.

Nursery tubes

The tiny tubes inside Steve's testicles are lined with cells that turn into sperm. Altogether the tubes produce some 3,500 sperm each second.

Sperm stay in the nursery tubes for at least two months while they practice swimming and become fertile (able to fertilize an egg).

Growing up

The tube where sperm mature (the epididymis) would be about 20 ft (6 m) long if it was stretched out. But coiled up on top of each testicle, the tube fits into a space the size of a bean.

"265 million, 381 thousand, 291—haven't we counted enough for one day?"

Reproduction

The penis is used to deposit sperm at the entrance to a woman's womb. A single sperm can merge with one of the eggs that a woman's body produces each month. The sperm fertilizes the egg, which grows into a baby inside a woman's womb.

Vas deferens

"They look just like tadpoles!"

"Yes, but a sperm is a thousand times smaller than a tadpole. It is only about 1/500 in (1/20 mm) long."

"Move along please!"

Epididymis   *Urethra*

"If Steve could get all the sperm he produced in one day to stop wriggling and line up, they'd form a line 10 miles (16 km) long."

"No! Steve needs a lot of sperm because each one has less chance of fertilizing an egg than I do of winning the lottery!"

Sexual intercourse

The penis is normally limp. But when it fills with blood, it grows longer and harder, and becomes erect. An erect penis is stiff enough to insert into a woman's vagina during sexual intercourse. At the climax of intercourse, muscles at the base of the penis squeeze rhythmically. This action, called ejaculation, forces semen out of the penis and into the vagina.

Urine control

A short tube connects the bladder to the hole at the end of the penis. Two sphincters (valves) control the flow of urine along the tube. Steve learned how to control these sphincters when he was a small child. He opens them to urinate (pp. 14–15).

"What a relief! It's yellow again. Steve ate too many beets yesterday and his urine turned pink!"

Making a vast difference

A muscular tube called the vas deferens links the testicles to the penis. During sexual intercourse, the muscles squeeze the tube to move sperm rapidly along it.

Sperm transport

Two glands just above the penis produce semen: a sticky fluid that nourishes, protects, and transports sperm when they leave Steve's body.

"Tight underwear makes Steve's testicles overheat and produce fewer sperm."

Testicle

Epididymis

Vas deferens

"Don't worry! Just follow the flow. I'll spot you when you splash into the bladder!"

"Each drop of semen carries a million or more sperm."

Being outside Steve's body keeps his testicles cooler then the rest of him—the ideal temperature for sperm production.

"Get a move on! We've got to pack 36 ft (100 m) in there!"

Prostate gland

A special muscle wrinkles the scrotum when Steve is cold, pulling his testicles closer to his body to keep them warm.

Scrotum

A woman's reproductive organs

The reproductive organs of a woman—the womb, ovaries, and vagina—are inside her body. Mature eggs travel from the ovaries to the womb. If fertilized by a sperm, an egg embeds itself in the womb and grows into a baby.

"In contrast to men, who make millions of sperm every day, a woman's ovaries usually produce just one mature egg each month."

Ovary

Fallopian tube

Womb

Fallopian tube

"The vagina is a tube leading to the womb. It provides a way in for a man's sperm to fertilize an egg, and a way out for a child during birth."

During intercourse, sperm swim up the vagina, through the womb, and along the Fallopian tubes, in search of an egg.

Vagina

A mature egg enters the Fallopian tube.

Ovary

A woman's ovaries contain some 300,000 egg cells. Each month one develops and travels down the Fallopian tube leading to the womb.

The heart

CLINGING TO A GLUCOSE MOLECULE, we surfed along Steve's veins. Eventually, the blood splashed into a rounded room. No sooner was it full of blood than a drain opened in the floor, and the walls closed in, forcing the blood out. We were in Steve's heart! It was no bigger than his fist, but powerful enough to squeeze 75 times each minute. It works like a pair of pumps. Each has two chambers. The lower chambers, called ventricles, do most of the pumping. Above each one is an atrium, which works as a temporary blood store. One-way valves at the exit from each atrium and ventricle stop blood from flowing backward. As the atria contract, followed fractionally afterward by the ventricles, the exit valves close making the relentless "lubb-dupp" beat.

Left or right?
Perhaps you are wondering why the right side of the heart is on the left-hand side of the page? Think about it. When Steve is facing you, on which side do you see his right hand?

1. At ease
At the start of every cycle of the heartbeat, the muscles relax momentarily. Blood pours into the right atrium. As the atrium contracts a three-pointed valve opens and blood surges into the right ventricle.

"We're the timing team. The electrical impulses we create travel down conducting fibers to keep the heart beating in perfect rhythm."

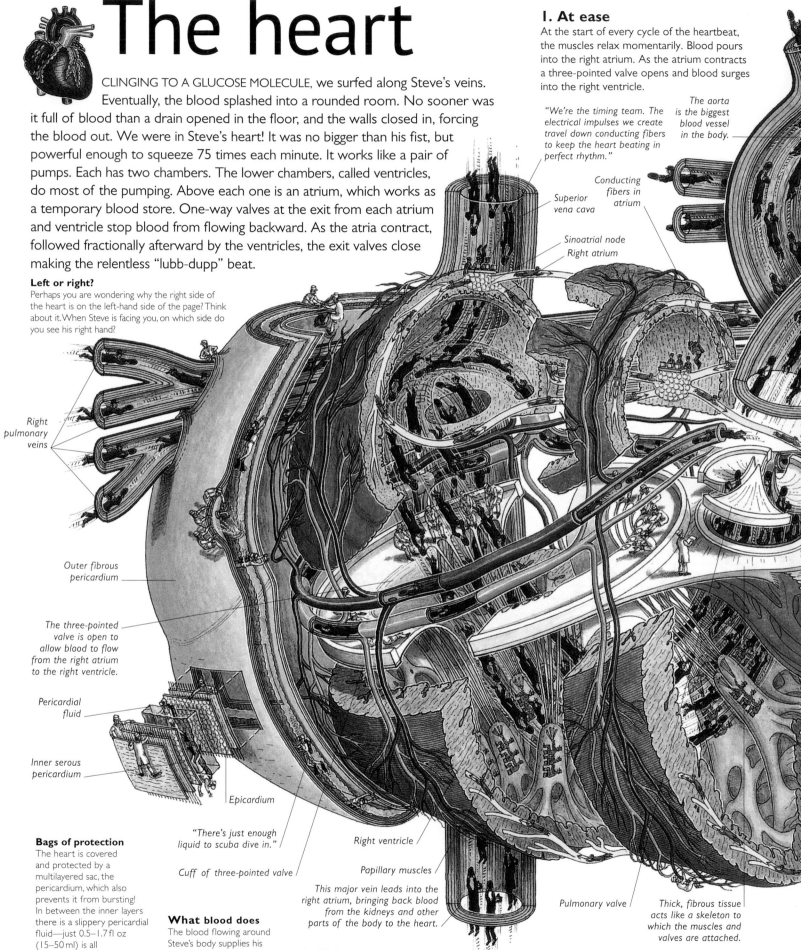

The aorta is the biggest blood vessel in the body.

Conducting fibers in atrium

Superior vena cava

Sinoatrial node
Right atrium

Right pulmonary veins

Outer fibrous pericardium

The three-pointed valve is open to allow blood to flow from the right atrium to the right ventricle.

Pericardial fluid

Inner serous pericardium

Epicardium

"There's just enough liquid to scuba dive in."

Cuff of three-pointed valve

Right ventricle

Papillary muscles

This major vein leads into the right atrium, bringing back blood from the kidneys and other parts of the body to the heart.

Pulmonary valve

Thick, fibrous tissue acts like a skeleton to which the muscles and valves are attached.

Bags of protection
The heart is covered and protected by a multilayered sac, the pericardium, which also prevents it from bursting! In between the inner layers there is a slippery pericardial fluid—just 0.5–1.7 fl oz (15–50 ml) is all that's needed.

What blood does
The blood flowing around Steve's body supplies his tissues with the oxygen and nutrients they need to live, and carries away waste products. It also contains substances that influence the temperature of his body, and contains cells that fight infection.

In full flow
At each beat, Steve's heart pumps about 3 fl oz (90 ml) of blood. That's about a soup bowl full every three beats. Blood vessels channel the blood around. There are two types. Arteries carry blood out from the heart. It returns to the heart along another set of tubes called veins.

2. Squeeze!
Next, the three-pointed valve closes and the right ventricle contracts. This pushes blood out through the pulmonary valve into the arteries leading to the lungs. The lungs remove carbon dioxide from the blood and replenish the oxygen supply.

Blood gushes out of the arch of the aorta through three arteries to travel to the head and body.

"We're delivering red blood cells. When they come back from the lungs charged with oxygen, the cells are bright scarlet. On their tour of the body the cells give up the oxygen and change color. They return to the heart a duller color."

3. Back from the lungs

It takes about six heartbeats for the blood to go all around the lungs and return to the heart. When the heart muscles relax, blood, rich in oxygen from the lungs, whooshes into the left atrium. Blood gushes down from the atrium through the mitral valve into the left ventricle.

4. Squeeze again

The right atrium squeezes a fraction before its partner on the left. When both atria squeeze, they force blood down into both ventricles.

5. Squeeze harder!

Finally, the mitral valve shuts and the left ventricle contracts. This forces blood up and out through the aortic valve into the aorta. From there, the blood flows on to supply the rest of the body.

The pulmonary arteries are the only arteries in Steve's body to carry deoxygenated blood, rather than oxygenated blood.

Aortic valve

Left atrium

Mitral valve

The heart muscle has its own blood supply. It flows along the coronary arteries, which branch off the aorta just where it joins the heart.

Powerful pumper
Steve's heart is fantastically strong and reliable. Each day it pumps enough blood to fill 70 bathtubs. When Steve is around 75 years old, his heart will have pumped 4 billion times.

Left pulmonary veins

Deoxygenated blood from the heart muscle returns along the great cardiac vein.

"Careful, the pericardium is slipperyyyeee!"

Left ventricle

"We pull on these fibers to stop the mitral valve from turning inside out."

Descending aorta

"We carry the electrical timing impulses along this special conduction system. But don't worry, we aren't in any danger of getting an electric shock, it would take a quarter of a million hearts to power a flashlight."

"This big valve is called the mitral valve because it looks like a miter— the funny hat that bishops wear."

Fibrous tendons

Independent muscle
The muscle wall of the heart is called the myocardium. It's unlike any other muscle in the body. If it were left to beat on its own, without input from the brain, it would beat at about 100 beats a minute. However, nerve impulses usually slow it down to about 75 beats a minute, and can slow it down or speed it up as necessary.

Fibrous skeleton

Nucleus

"That crowd on the right are a bunch of slackers. They only have to pump blood around the lungs. Here on the left we have to pump blood around the whole body. That's why the muscles on the left of the heart are much thicker than those on the right."

The nose and lungs

CLINGING TO A CARBON DIOXIDE MOLECULE, we rode the frothing red tide right through Steve's pulsing heart and beyond, into a wide pipe. The pipe divided into two narrower tubes, then forked again, and again, until the tube was almost too narrow to squeeze through. The noise of rushing air was almost deafening: we were in Steve's lungs. These two spongy bags almost fill his chest. His windpipe supplies them with air from his mouth and nose. Each branch of the airway ends in a tiny air-sac, surrounded by blood vessels. Here, deep in the lungs, Steve's blood exchanges poisonous carbon dioxide gas for life-giving oxygen. Steve's respiration (breathing) ensures a regular supply of fresh air. Inhaling (breathing in) fills the lungs with fresh, oxygen-rich air. Exhaling (breathing out) discharges the stale air and allows Steve to talk, sing, shout, and tell terrible jokes.

This stamp-sized area in the roof of Steve's nose cavity gives him a sense of smell.

Warm, slimy maze
Behind Steve's nose is a cavity that acts as an "air conditioner" when he breathes in. Its surfaces are warmed by blood and covered in mucus (snot). The air that flows over them is made ready to enter the lungs—it gets warmer and damper, and the mucus traps any dust.

Voice box
When Steve breathes out, air passes through his voice box. To talk or sing, Steve tightens muscles to stretch his vocal chords (flaps of skin) in the path of the air. The chords vibrate, making a sound. The tightness of the chords changes Steve's pitch of speech.

Steve's voice box is visible on his throat—it's known as his Adam's apple!

Vocal chord

Windpipe

Breathing muscles
Narrow strips of muscle link Steve's ribs. By tightening them, Steve lifts his chest and makes it bigger. This helps lower the air pressure in the lungs, drawing fresh air in through his nose and mouth. Normally, Steve only needs to relax the muscles to breathe out. However, when blowing up balloons he takes an extra-deep breath and forces the air out, making the muscles work harder.

Windpipe
A broad windpipe channels air from Steve's mouth and nose into his lungs. It divides into two tubes, the right and left bronchi, giving each lung a separate air supply.

Clavicle (collar bone)

"The muscle team makes Steve's breathing amazingly versatile. If he goes for a run, we work 25 times harder than when he's taking a nap."

Muscles connecting ribs

Rib

Chest muscles

Lightweight organs
The word lung comes from a Greek word meaning "light." Because of the air they contain, the lungs are the only organs of the body that are light enough to float in water.

Blood supply
The right side of Steve's heart pumps blood to the lungs along a wide artery. This divides into smaller and smaller branches, to form a network of tiny blood vessels that carry blood to each air-sac.

Pulmonary veins

Pulmonary artery

Veins
Tiny veins carry oxygen-enriched blood away from the air-sacs. They merge to form bigger blood vessels, piping the blood back to the left side of the heart, which pumps it on to the rest of the body.

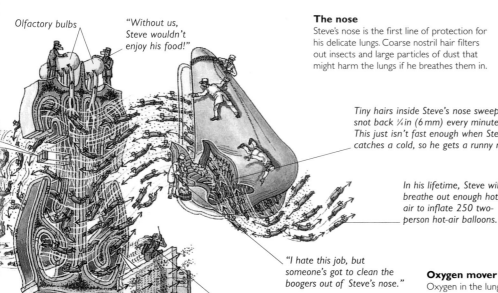

Olfactory bulbs

"Without us, Steve wouldn't enjoy his food!"

The nose

Steve's nose is the first line of protection for his delicate lungs. Coarse nostril hair filters out insects and large particles of dust that might harm the lungs if he breathes them in.

Tiny hairs inside Steve's nose sweep snot back ¼in (6mm) every minute. This just isn't fast enough when Steve catches a cold, so he gets a runny nose.

In his lifetime, Steve will breathe out enough hot air to inflate 250 two-person hot-air balloons.

"I hate this job, but someone's got to clean the boogers out of Steve's nose."

Oxygen mover

Oxygen in the lungs combines with saucer-shaped red blood cells. The cells carry the oxygen around the body and release it where it is needed.

"Cells in the wall of Steve's nose constantly replenish the layer of snot. If Steve catches a cold, these cells produce masses of snot to try and flush away the infection."

A huge spread

To ensure that enough oxygen reaches the blood, the surface area of the lungs is vast—84 square yards (70m²). Spread out flat, the lungs would provide enough parking space for seven cars!

Swapping gases

The airways of the lungs end in minute air-sacs. Blood vessels supply each one. The walls of the air-sacs are thin enough to allow oxygen and carbon dioxide gases to pass through, but thick enough to keep back the blood. Waste carbon dioxide in the blood passes into the air-sac to be exhaled. Oxygen from fresh air Steve has breathed in passes the other way into the blood.

Branching air-ducts

The airways that lead from Steve's windpipe branch again and again, until they resemble an upside-down tree. They have far more endings than a tree, however. A large oak tree has about a quarter of a million leaves, but a human lung divides into millions of tiny air-sacs.

Alveoli (air-sacs)

"These blood vessels are only half the width of a red blood cell. How does blood flow through them?"

"Simple. The red cells are flexible. They change shape and squeeze through in single file!"

"Red" blood cells look purple when they reach the lungs. They turn crimson when they have been recharged with oxygen.

Bronchial tree

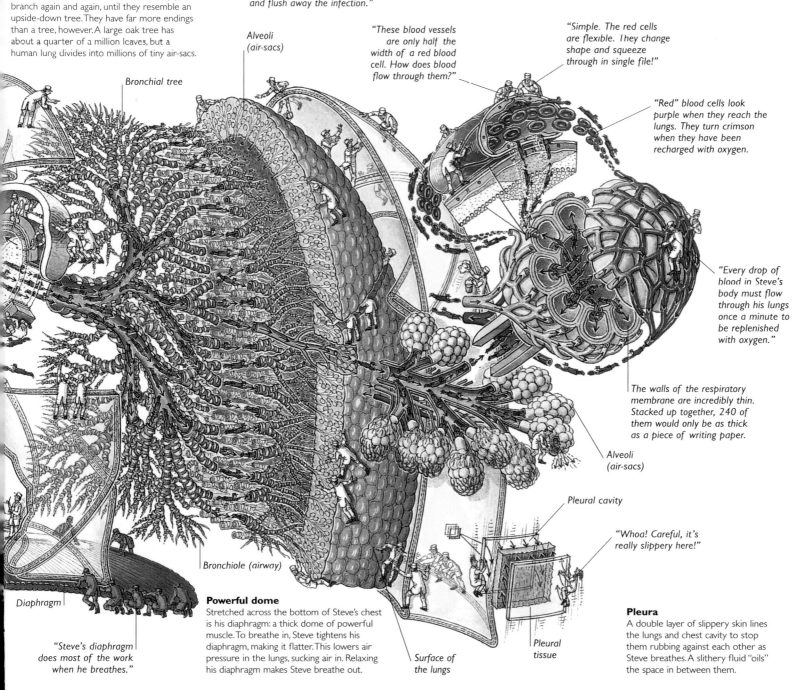

"Every drop of blood in Steve's body must flow through his lungs once a minute to be replenished with oxygen."

The walls of the respiratory membrane are incredibly thin. Stacked up together, 240 of them would only be as thick as a piece of writing paper.

Alveoli (air-sacs)

Pleural cavity

"Whoa! Careful, it's really slippery here!"

Bronchiole (airway)

Diaphragm

"Steve's diaphragm does most of the work when he breathes."

Powerful dome

Stretched across the bottom of Steve's chest is his diaphragm: a thick dome of powerful muscle. To breathe in, Steve tightens his diaphragm, making it flatter. This lowers air pressure in the lungs, sucking air in. Relaxing his diaphragm makes Steve breathe out.

Surface of the lungs

Pleural tissue

Pleura

A double layer of slippery skin lines the lungs and chest cavity to stop them rubbing against each other as Steve breathes. A slithery fluid "oils" the space in between them.

INDEX

ACKNOWLEDGMENTS

Dorling Kindersley would like to thank the following people for helping with this book:

Design: Joanna Pocock, Vicky Wharton; **Editorial:** Angela Wilkes, Anna Scobie, and Kathakali Banerjee; **Jacket:** Priyanka Bansal, Rakesh Kumar, Priyanka Sharma, and Saloni Singh; **Index:** Chris Bernstein